CARPENTER

"The only two legitimate sports are professional wrestling and roller derby."

CARPENTER

A PERSONAL LOOK AT PROFESSIONAL WRESTLING

DON SAVAGE

iUniverse, Inc.
Bloomington

Carpenter
A Personal Look At Professional Wrestling

iUniverse books may be ordered through booksellers or by contacting:

iUniverse
1663 Liberty Drive
Bloomington, IN 47403
www.iuniverse.com
1-800-Authors (1-800-288-4677)

ISBN: 978-1-4759-0702-5 (sc)
ISBN: 978-1-4759-0703-2 (ebk)

Printed in the United States of America

iUniverse rev. date: 06/01/2012

CONTENTS

PREFACE

It was not my intention in writing <u>Carpenter</u> to provide an expose on the professional wrestling business. I'd have to get in line to do that. I wanted to share some of my experiences over twenty years of taking bumps as a full-time/part-time wrestler. Some of these experiences were fun, some were not much fun, some were happy, and some were sad. In twenty years I met a lot of personalities, traveled many miles, and encountered good and bad situations.

I'm not prone to using profanity or vulgarity in my personal or writing vocabulary. I have quoted some of the people in my book verbatim so the language may be a little foul on occasion. I apologize, in advance, if this offends some readers.

I've tried to be as accurate as I can with regard to the spelling of the names of various individuals.

A pro wrestling terms glossary, located at the beginning of the book, will help the reader understand the language of the business.

Kick off your shoes, sit back, and I hope you enjoy <u>Carpenter</u>.

GLOSSARY

Pro Wrestling Terms

a.k.a.:   also known as.

Angle: the setting up for a future situation.

Apron: part of the ring platform outside the ropes.

Babyface: hero.

Belt: championship.

Blade: razor blade for getting blood during a match.

Booker: wrestling office executive in charge of personnel and setting up matches.

Booking: appearance date.

Bump: a fall.

Business: professional wrestling.

Called the match: gave instructions to my opponent.

Comeback: point where the babyface stops the villain and takes charge, at least temporarily.

Cover: pin fall.

DQ: disqualification.

False finish: cover, but only a "two count."

Finish: the conclusion of a match.

Going through: working the time limit to a draw (tie).

Heat: getting crowd reaction, usually negative.

Heel:	villain.
House:	paying audience.
House show:	live audience and no TV.
Job:	losing to one's opponent.
Juice:	blood.
Loose:	soft touch when working with one's opponent.
Mark:	someone in the audience, from whom we can get a reaction.
Married to:	working with the same wrestler on consecutive nights in different cities over a period of time.
Office:	management.
Off the top:	from the top rope or corner.
Pearl Harbor:	attack from behind.
Plant:	someone in the business who is planted in the audience to carry out an angle.
Potato:	a blow that accidentally makes hard contact.
Program:	build up a wrestler to stardom.
Put over/get over:	do a job.
Rib:	practical joke.
Set up:	placed in a questionable or compromising situation.
Shoot:	amateur wrestling.
Slab:	hard ring platform.
Snug:	not overly loose.
Solid:	real looking.
Squash job:	the carpenter doesn't make one comeback.
Stiff:	being tight or snug when working or a hard ring.

Territory: part of the country housing a specific wrestling organization.

Undercard: preliminary matches.

Work: staged "wrestling" compared to the amateur sport.

W.W.F.:   currently the W.W.E.

CHAPTER 1

So, You Want to Be a Wrestler?

When I graduated from college in 1958, I had six months before I had to report to the U.S. Navy to fulfill a reserve obligation (I played football for two years). What to do? Not wanting to get a regular job, I entertained the idea of pursuing professional wrestling. My parents had taken me a few times to the local venue in San Diego to watch a weekly card out of Los Angeles and I was fascinated by what I viewed—the lights, color, drama, the showmanship, and the group reaction to what was taking place in the ring.

I had wrestled a couple of years in college. I was a small heavyweight, and I wasn't very good, mostly due to lack of mat experience. Most of my opponents had been wrestling for years in youth and high school programs. I didn't start until eighteen years of age and that was a real disadvantage.

On a Tuesday morning I ventured down to the San Diego Coliseum on the corner of 15th and E and introduced myself to Ernie Fuentes, the local promoter. I told him that I wanted to wrestle. He informed me (lesson one) that the term was "work" not wrestle. I was six feet tall and weighed about two hundred twenty pounds. Ernie showed some interest although he knew I didn't know squat about the business. He directed me to return that evening for the weekly matches and meet a representative from the L.A. office.

Sandor Szabo was one of the bookers, along with Jules Strongbow and Charles Iwamoto (Mr. Moto) who operated the L.A. office. Tuesday night Ernie Fuentes introduced me to Sandor Szabo, a man of few words. He looked me over, gave me a wrestling license application, and instructed me to appear at the Saturday afternoon TV Wrestling Workouts at channel thirteen in Los Angeles. So, I did.

On the drive to L.A. I wondered what I might have gotten myself into and I had no idea what the format would be—not to worry. The boys welcomed me, and other than being extremely nervous, I felt pretty comfortable.

The format was a workout TV program with some angles to promote upcoming house shows. I was to workout with John "Broadway" Venus. When John and I shook hands in the dressing room, he could tell that I was a complete novice. "Let's go to the shitter and talk about a few things," he offered. In the ten minutes we were in the bathroom I learned enough to get through my workout with John. He was great—made me look as if I knew what I was doing. All I had to do was listen and follow his directions. The rest of the boys with whom I worked over the next three weeks were just as helpful.

After appearing on the workouts for three weeks, Szabo thought I might be ready for my first house match. After the Saturday workout, Szabo asked, "Any plans for tonight?" I responded with a no. "Good, you're in San Bernardino tonight." As I said, he was a man of few words. He finished up by telling me to get a name for myself—meet Don Savage!

Why Don Savage? My given name is Clark Staples—doesn't sound too athletic, does it? I wanted a name that could serve a "babyface" and "heel." "Don" was after Don Arnold, a San Diego product who had done well in the wrestling business. "Savage" was after "Crusher" Savage who was in the territory when I started. His real name was Ted Fainek, and he wrestled in the Navy while I was in college. Ted was not only a great worker but a pretty decent shooter. At one of the workouts, Ted and I rolled around with some amateur techniques. He pretty well dominated. He was preparing to leave the business, so I picked "Savage."

The true highlight of my wrestling workouts on Saturdays was meeting Lou Thesz, as well as Ed "Strangler" Lewis, and working with Thesz. He was a former world's champion (he held the belt for I don't know how many years). Lou was admired and respected by everyone in the business and possessed a fine sense of humor. During our workout, which lasted about eight to ten minutes, Lou took a side headlock and hip rolled me to the mat. On the mat Lou asked if I could hear him. I responded yes and looked forward to a high spot with the champ. "Are you sure you can hear me Don?" he asked again. "Yes," I said. "Good—how you doing?" he grunted with a chuckle. With Lou Thesz I really learned to listen, which is very important when you're new in the business. Legend and neophyte! Lou Thesz was a pretty "snug" worker when he took a hold or landed a forearm blow. It was felt—no damage, just "snug." And if an opponent mistimed taking a Thesz dropkick, it could be "lights out." Lou's legs were like pistons.

On another occasion, Lou and I were sharing a dressing room at the Olympic Auditorium in Los Angeles. I had already worked and Thesz was preparing for his match. He asked me to rub some lotion on his back. As I started to apply the lotion, I noticed it was Brylcreem and asked if he wanted Brylcreem on his back. Lou's response was, "Yeah, when you get to my age, its one tube for everything." There was only one Lou Thesz.

After my third Saturday on TV Wrestling Workouts, I packed my bag and headed for San Bernardino.

CHAPTER 2

Debut

Talk about nervous! On the drive from L.A. to San Bernardino for my first house match, all the things I'd learned from the previous three weeks on workouts flashed through my mind—was I ready for this? Listen carefully and follow instructions closely.

Tony Morelli, one of the "old timers" in the business, shared this thought with me. "Professional wrestlers are artists who paint a picture that is so easy to understand, the dumbest person in the arena can figure it out." Another Morelli saying was, "As dumb as we wrestlers are, the people in the audience are dumber—they paid to get in."

The San Bernardino Arena was relatively small. It seated about fifteen hundred max and it looked like a pretty good house, but not because of me. The main event was a return match with Buddy Rogers and Billy Darnell, two of the greats in the business.

My opponent was Dutch Schultz, a twenty year veteran in pro wrestling. Dutch was the heel; I was the babyface. His job was to talk me through the match, make me look good, and put me over—poor Dutch! Our match was one fall—twenty minutes and we were instructed to go for fifteen minutes with me finishing with two tackles and a body press: <u>KISS</u>—Keep It Simple Stupid!!!

Dutch did really well getting me through our bout. I could hear every word he said (the heel usually controls what goes on) and I followed every instruction. I learned a lot in that fifteen minutes and afterward in the dressing room debriefing. "Your punches are terrible! Start throwing forearms instead. Slow down and be more methodical. Remember, you're "telling a story" in the ring," Dutch advised me.

In my San Diego debut I worked again with John Venus and got my hand raised—two tackles and a body press. John paid me what I thought was a great compliment. "Savage," he said, "You've improved a ton since the workouts. Keep listening and learning." Thank you John!

The L.A. office used me two or three times a week until Christmas of 1958. The third of January was my report date to the U.S. Navy. Jules Strongbow was kind enough to give me a reference, if I chose to continue in the business. I'd had some promotional photos taken to go along with the reference in which Jules stated, "Savage is a fast learner." I certainly was still a rookie but I was starting to feel more comfortable in my matches. It was a good six months of learning the business.

CHAPTER 3

I'm in the Navy Now!

On January 3, 1959, I reported to the Navy Officer Candidate School at Newport, Rhode Island. Boy, was that a mistake! Classes, studying, marching, and classes, studying, and marching. I had just completed sixteen years of education, and I wasn't crazy about more classes or heavy duty studying. We marched to classes, to meals, and any time there were more than three of us in a group, we had to march, not walk.

I studied my butt off. I frequently requested early get up and late lights to study so I could keep my grades up. The toughest courses for me were navigation and ordnance (weapons). My math background was not that great; although, when I was in my forties I earned my private pilot's license which required math to a degree. It seemed easier then—maybe maturity?

My bunkmate was a graduate of M.I.T. He would study half an hour then leisure read. He sailed through the program; however, I marched better than he did.

About two months into O.C. School, word got around that the Navy had thirteen hundred candidates and only eight hundred available placements after graduation. Some super deals were going to be offered to thin out the herd.

What timing! On Friday nights each company held Field Day (barracks cleaning). I was in charge of the study hall detail, and I thought we did a great job. The place was spotless and ship-shape.

At personnel inspection Saturday morning, I experienced a terrible feeling—pencil sharpener! Had it been emptied and cleaned? Well, I broke ranks (got busted for that), and ran to our barracks (got busted for that too). Just as I was entering the study hall, the inspecting officer was emptying the sharpener shavings on the floor (bust number three in just fifteen minutes). That had to have been a record!

While the rest of Golf Company was on liberty in Newport, I was on the grinder for three hours of extra military instruction (EMI-Marching). Just into the third hour with only two of us still marching along with an EMI supervisor, a lt. commander approached and asked which one of us was C. Staples. "Here, sir," I responded not having a clue as to what he wanted with me. "Are you having fun Staples?" "No, sir," I replied. The officer studied me for a moment. "How would you like to pursue something more commensurate with your college background?" I still didn't know what was going on but for some reason I could sense "deal."

Within a week I was issued orders to report to Great Lakes Training Center for four weeks of boot camp, followed by ten days leave, and then on to Norfolk, Virginia, to complete two years of active reserve duty. Good-bye commission and hello football.

Boot camp at Great Lakes was somewhat of a comedy. I was in a company of sixty college graduates. Some with MA's and some with law degrees, but we all had one thing in common. None of us had enjoyed O.C.S.

We were isolated from the rest of recruit training command. Our barracks was located in an off-limits area. The only time we were with the other recruits was at meals. Our company commander had given us two basic guidelines: don't get in trouble and don't cause any problems. We spent most of the time playing cards and charades. We stood only one inspection, and I conducted it.

Fortunately our time in boot camp was brief—only four weeks. During the third week I met with a lt. j.g. who informed me that I was to report to Special Services, Norfolk, Virginia, in early May. He didn't say anything about football so I was still in the dark about what lay ahead.

CHAPTER 4

DOROTHY

Dorothy and Don in the late 1950's

In <u>Carpenter</u> I've tried to distance my professional life and my personal life. However, in this chapter, I want to spend some time telling you about my former wife, Dorothy.

Dorothy O'Loughlin was a year behind me at Chula Vista High School. Dorothy was beautiful, super intelligent, and probably the nicest person I ever met. I believe the only mistake she ever made was marrying me.

Dorothy and I dated for a while in high school and then went our separate ways. We were both at San Diego State in 1955 but didn't have much contact. In 1956 I transferred to Whittier College and earned my degree there, so we had no contact for two years. Dorothy pursued nursing and received her Bachelor of Science Degree and Registered Nurse Certification in 1959. In the fall of 1958 she was selected Homecoming Queen at San Diego State—a lovely queen indeed!

Late in 1958 we were both invited to lunch along with a few other Chula Vista graduates who had been high school friends. I was seated next to Dorothy and thoroughly enjoyed talking to her. I asked her out on a date and, surprisingly, she said yes. We shared our future plans and determined that we had a lot in common. One thing led to another and "boom," we were engaged! Even though things had moved rocket fast, Dorothy's parents and my parents were definitely in favor of our engagement and future marriage. Dorothy and I, along with our families, spent Christmas and New Year's together and then I was off to Navy O.C.S, and you already know that story.

During the ten days leave after boot camp, Dorothy and I were married—talk about rapid preparation! On April 30, 1959 we were wed at St. Rose of Lima Catholic Church in Chula Vista, CA. Father David Bailey officiated. David was a converted Southern Baptist and a very practical man. Knowing that I wasn't a Catholic, the only request David made of me was that I didn't prevent Dorothy from attending mass and I allow any children to be raised in the Roman Catholic faith. I didn't have a problem with that at all. I was brought up as an Episcopalian, and other than language (English/Latin), the services were somewhat similar.

The weather was unseasonably warm and the church was not air conditioned. As we stood before the altar, David noticed that I was perspiring somewhat profusely. He moved the microphone to the side and asked if we were okay. Dorothy and I both replied yes and David responded by whispering, "Good, it's hotter than hell in here." He retrieved the mike and continued, "Dearly beloved, we are gathered . . ."

Our folks did a great job of putting everything together and organizing the entire ten days.

After the wedding, Dorothy and I spent a few days in Laguna Beach, California on our honeymoon. I loved Dorothy and was happy we were married, but I was a bit unsure about the future.

CHAPTER 5

You Play Football?

I took an overnight flight from San Diego to Washington, DC and then connected to Norfolk, Virginia. There must have been a large group of sailors arriving at about the same time. A navy bus transported us to the receiving office at the naval station.

We stood in line with our orders waiting to be processed. When I was up, a receiving personnel man checked my orders, gave me a specialty selection sheet, and instructed me to designate "Special Services." I had no idea what Special Services was so I asked him. The personnel man studied me and remarked, "You're either a musician or a ball player. I would say ball player. You play football?"

I indicated that I had played high school and college football and had experienced a reasonable amount of success. At that point a gentleman dressed in civilian clothes entered the office. He was Bob Tata, the Head Football Coach and Athletic Director at the naval station. Coach Tata took over, got me processed, and delivered me to my quarters where I would be living for the next six weeks until Dorothy arrived.

For me, Special Services meant I was to play football from August to December and then serve as a physical instructor in the station gymnasium the rest of the year.

My duties in the gymnasium consisted of teaching a noon time fitness class which included exercises, running, team activities, as well as setting up individual workout programs for base personnel.

A truly rewarding experience for me was implementing a rehab/workout program for John Harris, a lt. commander who had undergone a cervical vertebrae surgery which had corrected the problem but left him with virtually zero strength in his arms and shoulders. John could not curl a five pound dumbbell. He was scheduled for a physical exam in a couple of months and was concerned that he wouldn't pass because of this lack of upper body strength. He was really concerned.

We started with two and one-half pound weights and worked on curls and lateral raises as well as presses. It wasn't easy for John; he endured a tremendous amount of discomfort to the point where tears would well up in his eyes, but he hung in there. He was an excellent example of "no pain, no gain." In six weeks, John could handle twenty-five pound dumbbells in all his exercises, and he did pass his physical—talk about rewards in teaching.

I was an offensive lineman, primarily a center—not big enough to play tackle or quick enough for guard—center it was. In high school I played only offense. In college I had to play defense as well because of limited substitution. In my two years of service ball, the NCAA was moving back to free substitution so I ended up playing only offense again which I thoroughly enjoyed with success. In 1960 I was selected to the All Marine Corps/Navy Team.

When I first arrived in Norfolk, I contacted Bill Lewis who promoted Norfolk for the N.W.A. (National Wrestling Alliance). I submitted my photos and Jules Strongbow's recommendation. Bill used me in Norfolk, Washington,

DC, and some shows in North Carolina, but the trips were relatively long with the exception of Norfolk.

About two weeks into our summer football workouts, I found out that the team trainer, Chief John Wareing, was a referee with the V.W.A. (Virginia Wrestling Association), a relatively small company that didn't really constitute a threat to either the N.W.A. or W.W.A. The V.W.A. ran shows in some of the smaller cities in Virginia: Petersburg, Hampton, Portsmouth, Richmond, etc.

I told John that I was in the business and showed him some photos. John took me to Hampton the following night and introduced me to Tony Olivas and Scotty Williams, the V.W.A. promoters, and shortly after that, I was V.W.A. property. Bill Lewis didn't seem to mind that I had changed companies. The thing that appealed to me most of all was short trips, and the money wasn't bad. We worked small arenas and attendance was pretty good. We had a TV show that promoted the various matches to be held in the territory.

I learned a great deal in my eighteen months with the V.W.A. We had a mixed group of talent. There were some older veterans who had attained star status with other companies and some young talent just getting started. It was a good blend.

John Wareing and I became good friends and frequently drove together. John was amazing. He was thirty-seven years old, five foot ten inches tall, weighed two hundred pounds, and didn't have any fat on him. He was in remarkable shape. On the football field he worked our butts off, and we were in condition to play in a short period of time.

In his younger days John was into feats of strength. He showed me photos of him holding back a Cessna aircraft operating at full power. Another photo showed John pulling

Garry Moore and his television show panel seated in the back of a pick-up truck using only his teeth. Folks didn't mess with Iron John Wareing!

When I started in the business, the California State Athletic Commission mandated that there was to be no blood in wrestling matches, so I didn't have any experience using a "blade." John educated me, showing me the proper technique for preparing and using a blade. Some of the boys carried their blade in their tights. Some taped it to a finger. I had the referee carry mine until I was ready to use it. When I said "juice" the transfer was made. The use of a blade to draw blood may sound a bit barbaric but it sure beats the hard way—punch, kick, etc. The first time I did my own blade job, I was working with Joe Romero in Hampton, VA. Joe took one look and said that there wasn't enough blood. He put me in a side headlock and drew a line across my forehead. I thought the entire front of my head was lacerated. In reality he had used his fingernail, which feels just like a blade, to have some fun with me—good old' Joe.

One time in Japan, during a blade transfer, the darned thing popped out of the ring. A ringside fan who, I guess, wasn't smart, simply picked up the blade and placed it on the ring apron. The referee retrieved it and we continued—go figure.

John Wareing was an excellent trainer. In my two years of service football, my only injury was a strained knee. John had me back in action in less than a week. I guess he believed in tough love because he didn't cut me any slack and the knee quickly returned to a hundred percent.

The last time I heard from John, he was an investigator for a private detective firm in Virginia Beach, VA. John's in his eighties now and I'm sure he's retired, although, knowing John, he may still be going strong.

I played my last service football game on December 4, 1960. I was released to inactive duty on December 8. Dorothy and I packed up our 1955 Chevrolet and with our six month old son, Bill, headed across the country to California. My plan was to pursue a teaching career and continue in the wrestling business.

CHAPTER 6

So, You Want to be a Teacher

When I got back to California, I was informed that I would need more course work to acquire my California teaching credential. I went back to school on a full-time basis. I contacted the L.A. wrestling office telling them that I would be available on weekends and vacations only. They booked me when they could.

I was told by a parent of one of my close friends that there was an opening at a private school in San Diego. The position called for teaching English (my undergraduate minor), and coaching football, basketball, and baseball. The job didn't require a credential. It wasn't going to pay a great deal of money but it would be a start. After an interview with the school's principal, I was hired to start the following September. Dorothy was already working at a local hospital as an emergency room nurse.

In July of 1961, I received a call from Tony Olivas, the V.W.A. promoter I had worked for back on the East Coast. He was now booking shows in Arizona out of Phoenix. I told Tony what my situation was and he invited me to work for him for a month. Things were starting to look up. It was a good month—short trips and the money wasn't that bad. I stayed in Arizona until mid-August and then returned to San Diego to begin my teaching career.

In 1961 and 1962 my wrestling activity was somewhat limited because I was teaching and coaching full-time as well as attending classes four nights a week to gain my California credential. The L.A. office used me when they could on weekends. They were running some Sunday afternoon and Sunday evening shows which fit into my schedule, so that gave me some work—thank you L.A. office. My first priority was to acquire the credential which I did in the spring of 1962.

In 1963 I was hired to teach English in the Grossmont Union High School District at El Capitan in Lakeside. The assignment also included coaching football and wrestling. Things were now going much better. I was involved in two activities, teaching and coaching, which were my career passions. I soon would be associated again with my third passion, the professional wrestling business.

CHAPTER 7

HAMMER AND NAILS—I'M GOING
TO BE A CARPENTER!

In 1963 I started getting back into the wrestling business "groove." The L.A. office used me on a regular basis—three and four bookings a week. It made for some long days—up at 5 a.m., to school for my morning workout (weight room and distance run), teach four classes, then my afternoon run (usually a timed mile), eat something, then off to that night's show in the car or a plane, depending on where I had to travel. I would return home at anywhere from 11 p.m. to 1 a.m. This was somewhat of a demanding schedule.

During the school's football and wrestling seasons, I would cut back some, but those sports were also time consuming. Thank God for youth!

One night at the Olympic Auditorium in L.A., Jules Strongbow met with me in private. I wasn't sure what he wanted, but Jules had always treated me well. He told me that I should entertain the idea of being a "carpenter." I didn't even know what a carpenter was. When I was with the V.W.A. on the East Coast, I was always programmed on top, working main events and semi-main events, usually three fall matches. I guess that represented star status and

I was getting my hand raised most the time. Being an "opponent" never entered my mind.

Jules indicated that as a carpenter/opponent I would be working with top talent in relatively short matches, and most of the time, early on the card, which would allow me to finish working and leave. He also pointed out that I had a full time job so being a carpenter would be an excellent way to participate in the business. It made sense. I didn't want to be a star. I just wanted a paycheck to supplement my teaching income. Turns out this was a good decision on my part because it was going to open a lot of doors in the future.

Operating as a carpenter, I was sent by the L.A. office to cities around the country to do jobs for a territory's super stars. It was fun and I got an opportunity to visit many places and meet a lot of interesting people. On occasion I became a little travel weary, but it was a great experience.

One summer I was scheduled to tour Australia and New Zealand for twelve weeks. The problem was the trip would have lasted three weeks into pre-season football workouts. I was still relatively new in the Grossmont District and didn't wish to create any "waves." I dropped the tour just to be safe (I'm still kicking myself in the butt for that decision). I guess two trips to Japan, visiting Canada and Mexico, as well as many cities in the United States somewhat made up for missing Australia and New Zealand.

Being a carpenter wasn't a bad way to pursue my wrestling career. I got plenty of work and the money was decent.

CHAPTER 8

JAPAN I: PAID VACATION

My first trip to Japan in 1965 was, in fact, an enjoyable paid vacation and lasted for eight weeks. We remained in the Tokyo area, and for the first four weeks, worked only Friday night television shows at Riki's Sports Palace. The last four weeks we worked two or three house shows per week. Each show paid bonus money over and above my contract and to be honest, I was getting somewhat bored working just one night a week.

I was with Johnny Kace and Paul Diamond and, during our time in Tokyo, we picked up some work as extras with the original "I Spy" (Cosby/Culp) production folks who were also staying at the Hotel New Otani. We spent most of our time waiting around but got into a few shots which I never saw because the show aired on Wednesday nights and I was always at the Olympic Auditorium for our weekly TV shows.

We became involved with "I Spy" when Sheldon Leonard, (long-time radio, film, and TV actor, and the executive producer of "I Spy") approached Johnny, Paul, and me in the hotel's coffee shop. He had read an article about Japanese men being "fondled" by Japanese women on the crowded trains and wanted to share with some Americans. During our conversation, one thing led to another and he hired us to work as extras in some shots. It was easy as we were already actors.

Johnny, Paul, and I were usually working tag match main events and single matches with Giant Baba, Yoshimura, and Endo who were the top Japanese stars and excellent workers. We had some great and fun matches over the eight weeks.

There was a group called the "Young Boys" who were basically new to the business and worked the undercards to our main events. Some of them became Japanese headliners over time and were offered trips to the United States.

One thing that the Young Boys had in common was that they were pretty stiff workers and blood (the hard way), was not uncommon in many of their matches. One kid whom we nicknamed "The Dentist" had a tendency to knock people's teeth out. I never had to work with him which didn't bother me at all.

Another of the Young Boys got our attention in a different way. We thought he looked like Oliver Hardy of Stan Laurel and Oliver Hardy fame. He was short, heavy, and wore a small box like mustache. He was a dead ringer for Hardy. It seems he was always injured and couldn't work, and his explanation was, "True dedication to the business." He was a nice guy with a great sense of humor. We named him "Ollie." The word was he left professional wrestling and became one of Japan's top show business comedians. He was a natural. On my 1971 trip to Japan, I encountered Ollie again and, indeed, he was an entertainment super star and married to a beautiful young lady. Go, Ollie!

The Young Boys also displayed an interesting concept with regard to verbal expression. They played a board game which was extremely popular in Japan. I assumed the Japanese don't swear or curse in their own language because while they were playing this board game, I would hear "son of a bitch" or "shit" or "bastard" from one of them, and then the conversation would continue in Japanese. I guess it was our western communication influence rubbing off on the Asian culture.

On both trips to Japan (1965 and 1971) I lost weight. I called it the "Japan diet." When I left the States, I weighed two hundred thirty five to two hundred forty pounds. When I returned, I was one hundred eighty five to one hundred ninety pounds! The only reason for the weight loss, as far as I can determine, was the heat and humidity, and I consumed a lot of rice—tons of rice. I drove the Japanese people crazy when I put catsup on my rice. I loved it!

I stayed away from their steaks, excellent Kobe beef. I was accustomed to barbecuing meat with lots of seasoning. The Japanese didn't season their beef. To me it tasted somewhat bland although the cuts were of outstanding quality.

One night at the Hotel New Otani dining room, I ordered fried prawns. The shrimp came with the heads on and I have a tough time eating food that's looking at me—back to rice.

My 1965 Japan trip was a pleasurable adventure. I saw a lot of their beautiful country and learned many things about the Japanese culture. In addition, I made some very good money.

"I thought the Japanese were supposed to be small people"—Giant Baba—7 feet tall and 300 pounds.

"Choking? Not me!"—Baba and Savage

Johnny Kace, Paul Diamond, and Don
Savage arrive in Tokyo, Japan.

"Autograph...anyone"?

"You want us to do what?"

"Take that, Japan!"—Yoshimura and Savage

Johnny Kace and Don Savage—"Bring on Giant Baba!"

Paul, Johnny, and Don introducing themselves to Giant Baba

CHAPTER 9

Japan: The People

One of the most enjoyable features of both my trips to Japan was meeting the Japanese people—super folks! They were friendly, polite, and eager to be of assistance.

I had more opportunity to interact on my 1965 trip than the 1971 tour because of our hurried schedule on the tour.

On the first trip, John, Paul, and I were presented bouquets of flowers at the airport, at our press conference, and when we arrived at the Hotel New Otani, which would be our home for the next two months. The following morning, I woke up at 4:00 a.m. after not sleeping very well. There were so many floral arrangements in my room I thought I was dead and in a funeral parlor. I couldn't get back to sleep so I decided to get some running in. Dressed in my warm-ups, I approached the hotel's front desk to inquire about some place where I could jog. The desk clerk promptly escorted me out of the hotel and down the street to Sophia University's quarter mile dirt track. I thanked him and put in a couple of miles on my new running facility which I would visit frequently during the next eight weeks. That desk clerk went out of his way to ensure that I had a place to run.

Another example of Asian hospitality: A young Japanese lady who worked in the hotel's tour office became our friend. She was engaged to a U.S. Naval officer and going to be married in the fall. Akio would meet us at breakfast on Saturday mornings and translate the newspaper coverage of our matches Friday night. She couldn't understand why we were always the "heels." Akio was a delightful person and fun to talk to.

One Saturday morning our sports page interpreter appeared at breakfast totally distressed to the point of tears. One of the hotel's guests, an American, had booked a tour with Akio the previous day, and some events on the tour were not to his liking. He proceeded to take out his issues on her in an extremely crude way—shouting profanities and basically making a complete jerk of himself in front of other guests. It wasn't a discussion; he was venting his rage on our friend.

John, Paul, and I asked if there was anything we could do to help. She declined our offer and thanked us for our support. That was not good enough! This asshole was totally out of line and making Americans look bad. That was our job as heels in the ring.

Time for a plan was in order. Obviously, we couldn't assault the guy, so we had to come up with something else . . . hmmm.

That night John and I set out on our revenge mission. We couldn't locate Paul so Johnny and I acted on our own. After midnight we rendezvoused in the hotel lobby. Kace had somehow gotten this turkey's room number—I didn't ask. Off we went to his floor. Upon arrival, we searched for a large potted plant. Actually, it was a tree and it was huge. It took all the strength we could muster, but we muscled this giant to Mr. America's door and placed it precisely where no one could get through either way. Hopefully we had the correct room and there wouldn't be a fire that night.

Strangely enough, we didn't hear any rumblings about that night's "agricultural field trip," but the following Saturday morning, our tour gal smiled and said, "Thank you." I guess we made our point.

The Otani's desk clerk and Akio were just two examples of the Japanese hospitality. There were many more during our stay in their country.

A rare time that I encountered Japanese hostility was on August 6, 1965, the twenty year anniversary of the Hiroshima atomic bomb attack. It was Friday night TV at Riki's Sports Palace. Johnny, Paul, and I were working with Giant Baba, Yoshimuro, and Endo in the six man tag match main event.

As usual, attractive Japanese models were to present us with flowers in the ring before the match. However, that night instead of accepting graciously, we were directed to throw the bouquets to the mat and stomp on them with contempt and disgust—ugly Americans! The promoters threw us a real curve. Instead of adult women, beautiful little five or six-year old girls were substituted. They were adorned in colorful kimonos and were absolutely adorable. My own daughters were about the same age. Johnny, Paul, and I all looked at our boss at ringside and he indicated to trash the flowers. Down to the mat they went followed by a severe stomping. The little girls were terrified and fled the ring in tears—so much for positive international relations.

Our pre-match activity had already created some pretty good heat with the audience. During the match, the three of us had Baba on the floor outside the ring. We were putting the boots to him when "wham"; I was struck on the back of my head by something. I reached back reacting to the blow and sure enough—blood the "hard way." I didn't have a clue as to what had happened. We finished the match and in the dressing room I was treated for a small laceration—nothing serious.

I didn't discover what had taken place until we viewed the tape back at the hotel. An elderly Japanese fan had come from the back of the arena, removed his gata (wood sandal) and bopped me with it. He then proceeded to sprint out of the Sports Palace. I guess my ring actions had a tendency to annoy him.

The only other aggressive person I encountered was our van driver, a diminutive man who was responsible for our local land travel. He was called "Caesar" and he did rule over vehicle traffic in and around Tokyo. With "Japan Pro Wrestling" printed on the van, cars did get out of his way. The only English I heard him speak was "Sunday driver!" When he was admonishing other car drivers, Caesar got us to our destinations in a hurry and it was fun to watch him deal with traffic.

It's been said that "people make a country what it is." I thought the Japanese did a fine job.

CHAPTER 10

Japan II: The Tour from Hell!

In chapter eight I indicated my eight weeks in Japan in 1965 were much like a paid vacation which was outstanding as far as I was concerned. There was enough work to keep us from being bored and an opportunity to leisurely travel the country.

In 1971, my second trip, I learned that Japanese television technology allowed the promotion to tape our house shows on the road and send the footage back to Tokyo for Friday night TV. This translated into a tour of Japan that was going to be a killer—twenty-eight days with twenty-eight shows. It would have been twenty-nine bookings but one ball park show was rained out.

What an itinerary—travel, work, travel, work, and sleep and eat when we had a chance. There were eight of us on the tour and at the conclusion, we were all "worked and traveled out."

The 1971 tour group consisted of Jack Briscoe, George Steele, Chris Markoff, Art Michalik, Victor Rivera, Mighty Igor (Dick Garza), Fidel, and me. Briscoe, Markoff and Rivera hung out together most of the time. Steele, Michalik, and I associated as a threesome socially. Igor and Fidel pretty much did their own thing. We all got along with each other and traveled well together which was important because we did a <u>lot</u> of traveling—planes, trains, and automobiles.

On many occasions we stayed in Eastern style hotels which meant sleeping on floor beds (futons?) and eating in Asian food restaurants, a new experience at first, but soon got old. I'd give my soul for a cheeseburger!

Many of the indoor venues we worked in were not air conditioned. They had fans but with the summer heat and humidity, the fans didn't accomplish much. In addition, the over the ring lights and TV taping lights made it pretty uncomfortable when we were working. Most of the Japanese spectators had their own personal fans which they used throughout the show.

One redeeming concept was the tubs of ice cold beer that the promotion provided for us when we completed our matches. Asahi, Kirin, and Saporo Beers were welcomed rewards in those ninety-five degree situations. Too many times we were buzzed or close to plastered when we boarded our next booking transportation or were deposited at our lodging for that night. I think that got me on the way to becoming a beer drinker.

At around twenty bookings into the tour, fatigue started to catch up with us. Between work and travel, we didn't have much time to just relax. Everything was according to "schedule" and the "schedule" was wearing us down. I believe I was getting a little homesick, wanting to have a night off and be with my family. It wasn't going to happen, and so on to our next destination. I began counting the days until the tour's conclusion and just hoping that there wouldn't be an extension for some reason. I remember one night at an outdoor show, Dick Garza (Mighty Igor) stood in the middle of the ring and screamed, "I want to go home; I don't like it here!" The pace was getting to him also.

At one outdoor show in Southern Japan, there was a moth infestation. There were millions of them. The mat was covered with them but the show went on. We did our thing, crunching the little critters moving around the ring, and taking bumps. A shower never felt so good.

On our last tour booking in Osaka, before returning to Tokyo, a Japanese physician friend of Art Michalik's invited us to his home after our show. Art had met him during a previous Japan trip. The Doctor and his wife were hosting a late evening dinner party for some friends and extended the invitation to Art, George Steele, and me. Their home was absolutely beautiful with manicured landscaping outside. The dinner was buffet style with Eastern food on one side of a serving table and Western food on the other side (as in steak, prime rib, ham, etc.). Guess where we lined up? Although, we did sample some of the Asian treats.

I don't think too many of the guests were into professional wrestling so other than our size and the fact that we were the only Americans in attendance; we didn't stand out too much. It was an enjoyable party and a pleasant break.

I was really made aware of just how punchy we were becoming on our last night in Japan. We were waiting for our flight home at Tokyo International Airport. Art Michalik and I decided to visit one of the airport's bars to pass the time. The bar was crowded so Art and I grabbed seats at opposite ends about twenty feet apart. Out of the blue, Art yelled at me, "Hey Don, you know what's wrong with this country? Too many fuckin' Japs!" This was completely unlike Art, and I hoped none of the Japanese people at the bar picked up on his comment. No one said anything but I was embarrassed for both of us. I guess we were really ready to come home.

On our 747 flight back to the United States, I mostly slept but did manage to cry my way through a few chapters of Erich Segal's <u>Love Story</u>. I had seen the film so I knew it would be sad. I even fell asleep on the thirty minute connection flight from L.A. to San Diego.

The round trip from L.A. to Tokyo, by way of Honolulu, was about thirteen thousand miles. We had put in at least that many miles during our travels in Japan in just twenty-eight days. No wonder I was tired. When I got home, Dorothy informed me that I had to teach a three week summer school session in English the next day—no rest for the wicked. I did enjoy sleeping in my own bed that night dreaming about Japan II—the tour from hell, that was now over.

CHAPTER 11

GOD, I HATED THAT MASK!

I spent most of my wrestling years working as a carpenter. On a few occasions, the office put me in a mask and programmed me on top (the "Ax Man" and the "Executioner"). I hated the hood, but it was a change of pace.

Promotion was building me up for a match with Ernie Ladd and I was winning my matches as the "Ax Man." One night Bud Cody was doing a job for me in Long Beach. During the match, Bud was executing a flying beal toss on me. Guess what? In the middle of the maneuver, the darned mask came off and flew out of the ring. Someone tossed it back in and I put it back on and we continued. I won the match, but the secret was out. Don Savage was under the hood. People must have short memories because the following week, Ernie and I worked before a pretty decent house. Ernie defeated me and put an end to the "Ax Man."

On another occasion, in Hollywood, I was working as the "Executioner". I would usually remove my mask at the end of the night when I got into my car but that evening, for some reason, two guys decided they wanted to follow me out of the parking lot. They stayed on my tail until I got to the Santa Ana Freeway. There they dropped me and off came the hood.

Most of the boys in the business have worked in a mask at one time or another. Even in the dressing room, we wore the mask pulled up on our heads so we could quickly bring it down if someone who wasn't smart entered the room. The mask was not fun.

One night in 1966 I was booked into Compton, California, as the "Atomic Masked Maggot Man." It seems that a lady wrestler from Tony Santos' Boston area operation wanted to promote wrestling while she was here on the West Coast. As long as I'd been with the L.A. office we'd never run a show in Compton. The office furnished her with some talent and helped her set up the program.

I was to work with an African-American wrestler and get my hand raised as the "Atomic Masked Maggot Man"—obviously a heel. I was in Japan in 1965 when the Watts riots took place and somewhat apprehensive about walking into the building—a white guy in a mask. I arrived a couple of hours early and entered without the hood.

While I was getting checked by the Athletic Commission physician, a black gentleman, I asked him how close we were to the riot area. His answer was that the building we were in had been destroyed and reconstructed. I guess that was close enough!

Gorilla Monsoon was also on the card that night. Gino suggested I wear his cape (red with a black gorilla's head on it) into the ring with it inside out so only black showed. In addition, this new lady promoter wanted me to leap over the top rope on my ring entrance.

What happened next was pure slap-stick comedy, never to be forgotten, at least by me. As I hurdled over the top rope, the cape got caught on the rope and deposited me flat on my rear end in the middle of the ring. I was completely embarrassed but the people in the audience, which was mostly black, went crazy. They immediately loved me. After that entrance, I couldn't do anything wrong. Every time I would punch, kick, or gouge, they would cheer—go figure! I guess I gained popularity from the seat of my pants.

I believe that was the only time the office ran a show in Compton, and I never saw that promoter lady again. That show also marked the last of "The Atomic Masked Maggot Man." Thank God!

In the early 70's, Hardy Kruskamp, who was promoting Long Beach and San Diego, made a somewhat strange request of me. It was football season and I was coaching; the office used me sparingly on weekends if I was available.

Even though San Diego ran on Tuesday evenings, Hardy wanted me to come to the Coliseum in a mask and street clothes, rope off a section of twelve seats, and sit there speaking to no one. It was going to take up only a couple of hours, so I agreed. This ritual went on for three weeks. During my fourth appearance, Hardy instructed me to jump into the ring and attack one of the working wrestlers (I think it was Art Michalik). Security intervened and escorted me out of the arena. The word was that I was supposed to be an incognito Pedro Morales who was coming to the territory. That's all I know.

How some of the boys could work for extended periods of time in a hood, I'll never understand. God, I hated that mask!

CHAPTER 12

PRIORITIES

Dorothy and I separated in 1972 and the divorce was final a few years later. I'm going to have to take the rap on this one. Along the line it seems that I managed to get my priorities mixed up and it cost me a marriage to a very decent person.

Teaching, coaching, the wrestling business, and my family were four of my major responsibilities. Unfortunately, I approached them in that order. Dorothy and I didn't argue that much because I was never home. I was always involved in activities that occupied too much of my time, and when I was home, I wanted to socialize with our friends instead of concentrating on being a good husband and father. It always had to be _my_ way! All Dorothy desired was some quality time together, but I was selfish and not very understanding and sensitive to her needs. I wasn't a kid anymore and should have perceived what was happening. The great Don Savage was not a very good human being, but nobody could tell me that because I had my own agenda and I was going to pursue it come hell or high water. What a guy!

As I look back now, it's easy for me to recognize the mistakes I made with regard to my wife and kids, but hindsight is always 20/20. I got caught up in what I wanted to be instead of what I should have been—priorities.

Dorothy and I have remained good friends and our children have become fine adults and are doing well. Fortunately they take after their mother. When our marriage failed, we did a pretty good job of concentrating on the kids, and they became priority number one. Dorothy was and is an outstanding mother and it reflects in the way the kids have turned out.

Neither Dorothy nor I have re-married, and we both know we can count on each other when times call for it—a good feeling. I believe that I have mellowed in my older years and have a better perspective of what's important in life. Better late than never.

If there is a lesson to be learned in this chapter I guess it would be, getting priorities in their proper order according to what's important in the short time we have here on earth. If just one person can benefit by examining the mistakes I made, then chapter twelve is a worthwhile addition to this book.

CHAPTER 13

Rings: Good and Bad!

A professional wrestler's best friend is a good ring. During my twenty years in the business, I can remember only a few occasions where I sustained damage due to my opponent's actions—a knee from Swede Hansen in the back and a knee from Pat Patterson in the eye. Possibly both incidents were my fault—zigging when I should have zagged.

The major culprits were bad rings as in hard or unforgiving. In a good ring, one can take any kind of bump that he wants to. In a bad ring, serious injury can occur with even the basic bumps.

What constitutes a good ring? The platform or foundation is the answer. Permanent boxing rings were the worst. The platform was like a slab with padding on it. There was absolutely no give whatsoever and very tough on the body. The ring at the San Diego Coliseum was one of the worst. I think they built the ring and then constructed the building around it. Unfortunately, I worked a great number of times in that ring and my body is paying for it. Body slams, back drops, and other elevation bumps were absorbed by planting our boots on the mat at the same time our backs made contact. This reduced the impact to a degree, but timing was essential. A lot of the boys, including me, had one inch thick crape soles on our boots to absorb the shock. This helped some, but the trauma on our ankles, knees, and hips, I'm sure, was excessive over the years.

A good ring was usually portable. Portable rings were used in TV studio shows, and I don't think I ever worked in a bad one. Some were better than others, but all were a welcome relief from the boxing rings that were permanent structures.

Some of the portable ring platforms were suspended over cables; other platforms were spring loaded with a center coiled spring. Both concepts provided the give necessary for the big bumps—body slams, back drops, suplexes, etc.

The V.W.A. had its own traveling portable ring. Scotty Williams, one of the promoters, was responsible for transporting the ring, setting it up, and tearing it down. My first couple of months with the company, I volunteered to assist Scotty and I learned a great deal about a pro wrestling ring. The platform is the key to a good ring. Our platform consisted of four plywood sheets that measured sixteen feet by four feet each. The platform frame consisted of interlocking tubular steel sections eight feet long with sleeves in each corner to accommodate the four ring posts which were seven and one-half feet in length and served as anchors for ring stability.

The plywood platform sheets were suspended on crossing one-half inch cable strands that could be tightened or loosened with small turnbuckles and they determined how much give we wanted in the platform. For platform padding we used carpet pad which was all that was necessary because of the platform forgiveness. The ring platform was secured with a mat cover that was strung and fastened into the ring frame. The three ropes were spliced half inch cable strands that had been fed through fourteen feet lengths of plastic garden hose to provide protection from the cable. The ring platform was sixteen by sixteen feet with fourteen feet inside the ropes—a nice size for a pro wrestling ring. Today's giants might need some more room but, for us, the dimensions were very adequate. The four ring posts were inserted into the corner sleeves and secured. The ropes were already fitted with turnbuckles that hooked into eyes on the ring posts at two, three, and four feet heights. The Everlast corner pads were tied to the turnbuckles, and voila, we had an assembled wrestling ring.

Scotty and I could set the ring up in less than an hour and tear it down and load it on the trailer in half an hour. The longest pieces we had to deal with were the plywood sheets which could be handled easily by two people. I could move the fully loaded trailer by myself without a great deal of effort.

Over the eighteen months I was with the V.W.A., I spent a lot of time in that ring, and we never had a problem with it faltering. I got to know it pretty well and I did discover that with the proper impact, one of the top turnbuckles could be disengaged from the ring post eye—new angle! I put tape on that turnbuckle, and on several occasions, I'd release the turnbuckle, use it to attack my opponent, which got some good heat, killed time, and set up some finishes.

I worked in a great many rings over my twenty years and some two thousand matches. The largest was twenty-two feet and the smallest was twelve feet. Surprisingly, the elevated bump techniques were essentially the same. In a small ring you don't want to launch your opponent out of the ring. And in a large ring, if you're too far away from your opponent, the bump will be telegraphed. Tackles, back drops, scoop slams, arm drags, etc. should be executed within five feet of the ropes so that the "bumpee" doesn't have to run a half-mile to take the bump.

It got to the point where I could determine a good ring or bad ring as soon as I stepped through the ropes entering the ring. A creak meant a good ring and no creak meant a bad ring. I got to love that creaking sound.

Roy Shire, who promoted the California Bay Area, had a spring loaded TV studio ring that was fantastic. I could take any kind of bump I wanted. It was very forgiving! However, the first time I worked the Cow Palace in San Francisco, there was a different ring. This ring was pretty stiff and the platform was four feet high instead of the standard three feet. A bump over the top rope meant a drop of eight feet to the arena floor. Not too many of the boys went over the top!

I never worked in a ring that didn't have cable ropes as opposed to hemp ropes. I've seen boxing rings on TV that featured hemp ropes, and on a few occasions, the ropes parted or experienced some kind of problem that put a halt to the action while repairs were made. With cable ropes, I had only had one problem that I will relate to in my personalities chapter. The key to cable ropes is to relax the tension or disconnect them when they aren't in use. This allows them to remain taut when they are in use during matches.

Most of the mat covers were a soft heavy duty muslin that could be laundered regularly for sanitary reasons. Although the term "canvas" is commonly used, muslin was much easier on the skin in avoiding abrasions (mat burns) on elbows and knees. Muslin also seemed to provide a more comfortable surface than canvas.

Good rings are an important part of pro wrestling action and are also much easier on the body. They're not trampolines, but they're not slabs either. I, personally, would like to see boxing in wrestling rings in hope of reducing serious injury resulting from boxers' heads striking hard ring platforms which are quite common in most boxing only rings. I'm aware that punch damage is still potentially dangerous, but a forgiving ring might help out in some of those "timber" knock downs.

A good ring is an important tool in the professional wrestling trade. It allows better action with some fantastic bumps and isn't so hard on the wrestlers' bodies.

CHAPTER 14

DRUGS: COMEDY AND TRAGEDY

I was in high school and completed my college undergraduate work in the 1950's. The group with whom I associated at both levels were non-smokers and non-drinkers, and I didn't even know what "dope" was. I don't think I'd ever heard of marijuana. In college there was mention of some students taking "pill help" to allow them to study for long periods of time without having to sleep, but I couldn't pin point any specific individual.

At Whittier College where I spent my junior and senior years, it was an unwritten rule that nobody smoked on campus and if a student got busted for drinking any place, it was grounds for suspension or expulsion from school. That was then; this is now!

When I was playing service football (1959-60), I might have had a few beers now and then but I wasn't a real drinker. I was an occasional drinker and drugs weren't even in my vocabulary. It was 1960 where I personally encountered some form of narcotics. One occasion was some-what humorous and the other very sad.

Ron Lafferty, one of our offensive linemen, was sold on taking "pep pills" or "uppers" before a game so that he could perform at a "higher level." These pills were Benzedrine, Dexedrine, or some derivative of those medications. Ron was always trying to convince me that this was the way to go and I always responded with "Thanks, but no thanks."

In our 1960 season, we lost the opener to the Camp Lejune Marines but had won our next four or five games and were improving as the season progressed. In middle October we were the host team in the Good Neighbor Bowl at Foreman Field, our home game stadium. The Good Neighbor Bowl culminated a week of festivities celebrating the city of Norfolk, Virginia's municipal history, so it was an important game on our schedule.

The visiting team was Mitchell Air Force Base from Hempstead, New York, a team we had lost to in 1959 in a very close game.

Once again Ron Lafferty approached me about partaking. For some reason I decided to take the plunge and accepted his offer. I guess it was more curiosity than anything else. For me this was going to be a night to remember and deter me from associating with drugs any time in the future.

The game with Mitchell ended in a scoreless tie and later the films showed that I played just about my standard game. I did some things well and some things not so well, but that was just the beginning.

Dorothy and I hosted an after-game get together for a few of my teammates and their wives. We had beer, soft drinks, sandwiches, etc. We didn't get started until eleven p.m. and at about one thirty a.m., I could barely keep my eyes open. I was hinting to folks that it was time to go home because I was falling asleep on my feet. Finally everyone had left and I couldn't get in bed soon enough. I was looking forward to a good night's sleep—ha!

As soon as my head hit the pillow, it happened—my eyes closed and then I must have imagined a giant "flash" inside by head. Both eyes popped open and I literally couldn't close them. It was if they were stuck wide open and they weren't going to close. Even when I manually pulled my eyelids down, it was impossible for me to close my eyes—for the next ten hours! All night, and for the better part of the next day, my mind said sleep but my eyes wouldn't cooperate. It was a scary situation.

It took me a good two days before I stopped feeling the sensation of being "jumpy." Even though I didn't seem to have sustained any permanent damage, that experience was sufficient to let me know I wasn't going to try that again. Although at the time, my exposure to drugs wasn't too funny, the entire scenario was somewhat of a comedy as I look at it now.

My only other real encounter with narcotics was also in 1960. Dr. Jerry Graham and Johnny Valentine were the current top stars in the V.W.A. along with Pedro Morales and me. Many of the main events were tag matches featuring the four of us, and we had some pretty decent bouts.

One of the new wrestlers in the territory was a man named Ricky Columbo whom I had never met. He was friends with either Graham or Valentine and seemed like a good guy but, as I said, I didn't know him.

Ricky apparently had a problem with drug abuse—heroin. I should have known something was not right when I overheard part of a conversation between Ricky and Valentine. Ricky was almost crying and was probably hitting Johnny up for some kind of an advance so that he could acquire a "fix."

Ricky and I had worked together and he was a good worker. He was probably clean on those occasions. One time when we were tag team partners, he indicated that he wanted to throw-up to insert reality into our match. That kind of got my attention. Promotion denied his request so Ricky abandoned that idea—strange.

It was March in Richmond, Virginia, and the weather hadn't warmed up yet. Ricky and I were working together in a single match. I should have known that he was high on something. About five minutes into our match, Ricky had me in a back body scissors hold. Now the standard angle here is that I would try to unlock his legs to free myself. His response was that he would lock under my arms, elevate me from the mat, then bring me back down to the mat on my butt with a bang, and I would sell the bump. We did this bit once, and then it happened. Before we could repeat the move, I felt a sickening thud on the back of my head. I reached back to feel what had occurred and sure enough there was blood, the hard way and plenty of it. I thought Ricky had opened me up with a head butt but that wasn't the case. I heard him laugh and say, "You'd better cover me, Don," and when I turned to face him and do that, I was horrified at what I saw. That idiot had a laceration on his forehead that extended from his hairline to the bridge of his nose, and it was just gushing blood. In spite of some portable heaters that had been placed around the arena, it was still cold and I could see steam coming from the gash. It might have been my imagination, but there also seemed to be a foul odor associated with the wound. I almost lost my lunch.

I pinned Ricky and immediately left the ring to track down Tony Olivas, the promoter. When I caught up with Tony, I told him, in no uncertain terms, that if he ever booked me with Columbo again, I would resign from the V.W.A. Tony honored my demand. Ricky was treated at a Richmond hospital and required a ton of stitches in his forehead to close the wound. The only damage I sustained was a bump on the back of my head and Ricky's blood all over me.

Shortly after, Ricky Columbo left the territory, and the word was that in the next year or two, he passed away from either a drug overdose or suicide. I guess the demons that tortured his life, took his life, and maybe Ricky finally found some form of peace.

In the late 1980's, when I was counseling at Santana High School, I received a call from the Adult School office. They had a student who was high on meth and climbing the walls. Adult School wanted me to talk him back to reality—fat chance! With the help of paramedics, we restrained the kid and got him transported to the hospital. What a great opening to my workday!

To this day drugs still scare me, and I don't want to have anything to do with them. We have enough problems in the world; narcotics don't solve problems, but they sure can create some.

CHAPTER 15

FOOTBALL PLAYERS IN WRESTLING TIGHTS

It's a fairly difficult transition to move from an activity that requires a full output of energy (football) to one that emphasizes control and restraint (professional wrestling). Some people are successful at making the transition and others aren't. I have seen both ends of the spectrum during my years in the business.

The great professional wrestlers possess skills that make them stand out at what they do. Creativity, timing, development of a persona which individualizes their character, and hard work and dedication are some of the qualities that put them on top.

One of my English students who, in my opinion, was close to world class caliber in gymnastics and exhibition diving had all these qualities. I watched a few of her competitions. She not only demonstrated complete control of her body movement, she reflected a presence of perfect self-control and purpose. It was a pleasure to view. The only downside was, she was seventeen going on eighteen, and the world class kids were thirteen to fifteen years of age. I believe, if this young lady had trained at a very early age with coaches at the international level, she would have had a good chance to compete for a possible spot in the U.S. Olympic trials. What she did, she did exceptionally well.

I think the same concept applies to the wrestling business. A person can be big, strong, and quick, and not be a good football player. It takes a certain type of athleticism, technique, and desire to be successful in any sport. The same holds true in professional wrestling, and that's why some of the boys make it to star status and others don't. I was one of the "don'ts." Remember, I just wanted to receive a check and serve as a carpenter, not be a star.

Dick Beyer (The Destroyer) who was a captain on the 1953 Syracuse Orange Bowl Team made a very successful transfer from football to the wrestling business, as well as Art Michalik, Don Manoukian, Ernie Ladd, and Dick Afflis (Dick the Bruiser) because they were able to adapt and modify. I had played ten years of football, never at the professional level, but some good football, and I found it somewhat easy to transition. As an offensive Lineman, there were times when I had to be very aggressive (run blocking) and there were times when I had to be somewhat passive (drop back pass protection). This may have been of some help in moving to the professional wrestling format. I also had some great guys teaching and working with me, which made a big difference. I'm sure there were other football to wrestling athletes whom I didn't know who successfully made the switch.

I remember viewing a vintage tape of Lou Thesz working, I believe, with all-time football great Bronko Nagurski. I knew, from personal experience, that Thesz was a great, but snug worker and I imagine Nagurski was pretty stiff. It looked to me as if Lou and Bronko executed their throws and holds with extreme vigor with plenty of bumps and bruises to go around—a solid and super match well worth watching.

Professional wrestling demands special attention to great technique and precise timing. I believe some of the workers just come by these qualities naturally and others have to develop them over time with experience. Some of the boys I worked with didn't have a clue and never would. Hopefully, they found other ways to earn a living.

CHAPTER 16

COMMUNICATION IS THE KEY

Because the professional wrestling business is based on communication, it is extremely important to be a good listener and be able to express one's self quickly and accurately. Failure to possess these abilities could screw up high spots, finishes, and the whole match. I've seen this occur on too many occasions.

Any time wrestlers' heads are in close proximity, there is probably some type of communication taking place. For example, I have my opponent in a side head lock, I drop my head close to his and he says, "one tackle; get it again." This means he will launch me into the ropes; I will execute one tackle and then take the headlock again. Brief, but precise instructions. A wrestler taking instructions is somewhat like a football linebacker taking keys from what's happening on the line of scrimmage. He knows what reactions are required in certain situations.

Veteran Don "Hard Boiled" Haggerty would yell out his instructions. "Savage, you son-of-a-bitch, two tackles and get it again." I don't know how he got away with this technique, but he did, and I always knew exactly what he wanted to do.

About the only things we went over before the match was the finish and any special high spots or angles to be shot. The rest we covered in the ring during the match. The referee kept us apprised of time elapsed so we knew when to finish. On one of the Bay Area TV shows, the promoter sat at ringside with a pencil in his hand. While the eraser was up, we continued to work. When the lead went up, it was time to finish. The Olympic Auditorium in L.A. had a digital scoring clock so we could keep our own time.

Pro wrestling "lingo" is an interesting concept. The term "k faben" or "k fabe" alerts wrestlers that there is someone present who is not smart to the business, so watch what you say or do.

Another communication technique is what I call wrestling's version of "Pig Latin." I learned it in my early days in the business from one of the old timers, but I found there wasn't much of a call to use it.

It involves starting a word with its first letter or diphthong, then inserting "eaz" and concluding the word. Example: say becomes "seazay," them becomes "theazem," and wolf becomes "weazolf," etc. It's fairly easy to use when necessary. In his book, the great Freddie Blassie, indicates he was aware of this form of communication but he didn't really understand it. I wish I had known this when I worked with Freddie; I could have driven him crazy.

I found that most of the times I made mistakes in a match was because I didn't listen carefully enough or didn't communicate effectively. Communication is the key!

CHAPTER 17

Transition: Babyface to Heel

In the motion picture industry, actors sometimes wish to change their on-screen image. The same holds true in the professional wrestling business. There are new challenges, new techniques to be learned, and the development of a new persona. For some of the boys it came with ease to switch either way; babyface to heel or vice versa. Guys like Freddie Blassie, Johnny Valentine, and Buddy Rogers could make the transition by changing facial expression—a scowl to a smile. I once saw Johnny Valentine enter the ring as a hated man, and by the time he left the ring, he was applauded and cheered just because he performed a few decent moves and smiled at the right time. We're talking about a time period of fifteen minutes. I was amazed.

From 1959 to 1960, I had been working as a babyface in the V.W.A. I was on top most of the time, involved in mostly main events and semi-main events and doing well, with lots of bookings and getting my hand raised most of the time. It was enjoyable, but I was ready for a change. I liked the idea that heels directed the flow of a match, and babyfaces listened for direction.

I approached the promoter, Tony Olivas, with my intentions and fortunately the territory was a little heavy with babyfaces, so he went along with my suggestion. Now, how to make the transition.

It was a lot easier than I had imagined it would be. We were in Richmond, Virginia, and I was in a tag team main event with Scotty Williams as my partner. The angle was this: the opposing team, The Crippler and Von Hindenburg, had put the boots to me but I managed to escape and tag Scotty. Scotty made a brief comeback and then got caught and they took over on him. Von and Crippler had Scotty in a great deal of trouble but he was able to get in tagging range and I refused to tag in. Two or three more attempts were made by Scotty, but I would have nothing to do with him. Finally, I jumped down from the ring apron and proceeded back to the dressing room. Don Savage is now Don "The Coward" Savage. From that moment on, I was a certified heel, and it was fun most of the time.

There were advantages in being a heel. I called the match. It gave me the pleasure of getting heat with the wrestling fans and I thoroughly relished it when I was the victim of a high spot or a finish—all fun concepts.

There were also some disadvantages, not with the boys, but with a few fans with bad intentions. I was stabbed twice (to be covered in another chapter). Also, I had to always watch my back when I was in the audience's territory. You never know "what lurks in the minds . . ."

One skill a good heel develops is the ability to locate and work to certain "marks" in the house and get some good heat. I once worked a twenty minute match with Ox Anderson, a great heel for many years. Ox got so much fan heat on him that we didn't even touch each other for the first ten minutes of the match. It was a work of art and entertaining for me to watch. In addition, I was learning technique on rousing crowd reaction that would help me when I made the move from babyface to heel.

I believe it's important to know how far to go as a heel and when good judgment should prevail. It's impossible to read wrestling fans' minds and we were never quite sure with regard to which buttons to push and which buttons not to push. It's a gray area that sometimes can lead to dangerous situations.

In 1965 the L.A. wrestling office worked me five nights a week for three weeks to get me in shape for my first Japan trip. They knew that the heat, humidity, and Japan Pro Wrestling's demand for lots of action, bumps, holds, and a great deal of movement in and out of the ring would take its toll on my physical abilities. They were correct. Conditioning was important.

On Monday nights I was booked into the Pasadena Arena, a small and congested venue. I was working as a heel and, evidently, highly agitated one of the male fans—a real mark. I verbally abused him to the best of my ability with results. I really believe he would like to have injured me in some way. This is what a good heel wants—taunting the fans to the point of total frustration, and I had this mark to that level. Fortunately our exchanges remained verbal with no physical violence.

During my second week in Japan, I was informed that Benji Ramirez, who was working under a mask as "The Mummy," had been seriously injured at the Pasadena Arena. It seems that Benji had antagonized "my mark" to the point where there was a physical confrontation as Benji was making his way out of the ring to return to the dressing room. During the altercation, Benji was slashed by this damned wacko and required several stitches to repair the damage. I don't know what Benji did to generate this type of response but it's possible that he crossed the line. As I said, we can't read minds.

I did a job for Pompero Firpo "Wild Man of the Pampas" at San Francisco's Cow Palace one night. As he was going up the aisle to the dressing room, someone nailed him with a beer bottle. Firpo was accustomed to that kind of treatment from crowds that he infuriated, and he did know how to infuriate people. In fact, he was a master at it. After the attack, Firpo just bled and brushed the incident off, un-phased by what had taken place.

In essence, being a heel in the wrestling business can produce both good and bad moments but, above all, it can be an interesting and eventful challenge.

CHAPTER 18

STRANGE BUT TRUE

During my years in the wrestling business, I was either part of or witnessed some weird situations. All of these occasions reflected some form of human behavior that was sometimes entertaining, sometimes a little scary, but always interesting. In this chapter I will relate a few of these occurrences that definitely caught my attention.

Incident: 1959, Petersburg, Virginia. I was involved in a tag team main event with Alex Medina as my partner. Our opponents, whom I'd never met before that night, were an Asian (who was no more Asian than I was) and his partner, a young kid with a tremendous body and a funny look in his eye (strange—not ha-ha). As we went over the match in the dressing room, this kid maintained that look as if he wasn't quite sure where he was. To me, this was a little unsettling, but I didn't say anything.

The finish of the match called for this kid doing a "Pearl Harbor" move on me while the Asian kept Alex and the referee occupied. I was working the kid over in a corner; he reached back and snatched the wood ring post cap and wacked me with it. I went through the ropes to the arena floor, did a quick blade job, and got lots of blood. By this time, the ref's attention had turned to my predicament and he counted me out. Of course everyone in the arena, except the referee, saw what the kid did, and they were not happy with the outcome.

Covered with blood, I was assisted back to the dressing room and then the "crap hit the fan." The crowd evidently took exception to what had occurred, and rapidly became a "lynch mob" not letting the kid out of the ring. The Asian and the ref possibly sensed the potential situation and departed the ring A.S.A.P., leaving the kid by himself to face some hostile fans surrounding the ring—approximately one hundred in number. I thought the kid had been a fairly decent worker, a little raw because of his inexperience, but he didn't screw up high spots or the finish. Now it appeared that he was in trouble. That funny look in his eye had changed to a look of real concern, as if he were afraid for his well-being or possibly his life. He was flat out scared. I was in charge of running the matches that night and the local promoter was apprehensive about the situation getting out of hand with the potential for a riot. He approached me and ordered me to do something, pronto.

Still bleeding, I returned to the ring area pushing people out of my way, entered the ring, and grabbed the microphone. Inside I was thinking I sure hope this works. I gained the fans' attention and pleaded for them to allow me to take care of things in my own way. I proposed a no disqualification match the next week with the loser having to leave the territory. I also indicated that I wanted the kid to be left alone so that I could deal with him accordingly—"destroy" him. This seemed to appease the mob to a degree and they slowly backed off and exited the arena. Whew!!!

Back in the dressing room, the kid thanked me for what he thought was my saving his butt. The following week, I won our no D.Q. match and the kid either went to another territory or left the business. I never heard.

Incident: 1970, Ventura, California. I was working a single match with Art Michalik, putting him over after the fifteen minute mark. We were going to kill some time with the "concealed foreign object" bit. I took a top wrist lock on Art, and he used the object to reverse the situation, driving me to the mat—standard operating procedure so far.

A lady at ringside screamed out, "Ref, Boom Boom has something hard in his tights!" Johnny Dugan was refereeing, and he was the first to crack up. Art did the best he could to keep a grimacing straight face. I was lucky because I was lying on my back and the audience couldn't really see my face. It didn't stop there. This lady persisted, "Ref, look for Michalik's hard thing. It's in his pants!" Every time Art used the gimmick, this gal would sound off, "Ref, grab Boom Boom's hard thing." We finally gave up because we were losing our self-control. Johnny, Art, and I were in stitches, so I gained possession of the object and nailed Art with it. I guess this made the lady happy, and she shut up after that. We could then finish the match in character.

Incident: 1965, Tokyo, Japan. I was seated in the lobby of the Hotel New Otani awaiting our transportation pick-up for Friday Night TV at the Sports Palace. Johnny Kace and Paul Diamond hadn't come down yet.

There was an entourage gathered at the front desk. In the center of this group was a gentleman who looked like an athlete. He was ruggedly good looking, about six feet tall, maybe two hundred pounds, with a very noticeable scar on the bridge of his nose—a boxer?

Our transportation arrived and I forgot about the man. The next night I walked into one of the Otani's informal dining rooms and there he was, sitting alone at a table having his pasta dinner. I couldn't resist, so I approached him and introduced myself. My curiosity had won out. He was extremely cordial, shook my hand, and introduced himself as Renato Cioni from Italy. He spoke English with a pronounced accent but he was easily understandable. Renato invited me to sit down and he indicated that he was in Tokyo to sing the role of Lieutenant Pinkerton in Puccini's Opera, <u>Madame Butterfly</u>.

I had grown up in a classical music environment. My dad and older brother were into operatic and symphonic works, and I guess I picked up a lot through osmosis, enjoying much of what I heard. In fact, as a kid I wanted to sing Grand Opera and play football. During my junior year in high school, my voice had essentially changed and my parents arranged for me to study voice with Lee Whitney, voice coach and also vocal director with San Diego's Starlight Opera Company. At the conclusion of my audition with Lee, she told me that I had a nice voice, a good voice, but not the potential for a great voice. There would be no grand opera for me but my voice was suited for musicals and "saloon singing." I was disappointed but able to face reality and through the years I did do some shows and clubs when my schedule permitted.

Now here was I, a pro wrestling carpenter, sitting at the same table with a Metropolitan Opera tenor. What an experience!

Renato and I seemed to hit it off pretty well. We met for dinner twice when we both had nights off. On one occasion, I asked him how an operatic tenor acquired such a sizable scar on his nose. Renato told me that when he was a twelve year old in Italy, he made the mistake, at an evening meal, of helping himself to some bread before his father had said grace. Papa promptly launched a dinner plate across the table striking Renato squarely on the nose, causing a fracture with a lot of blood (the hard way). Papa regained his composure, apologized, but the damage was done. Renato could laugh about it now but I'm sure it was a frightening occurrence when he was a young boy. Lesson: Always keep an eye on old dad when at the dinner table.

Because of schedule conflicts, I didn't get an opportunity to enjoy a <u>Madame Butterfly</u> performance, but I did meet one of the stars, Renato Cioni.

Incident: 1965, Tokyo, Japan. A Continental Air Lines crew was staying at the New Otani on their layovers. One of the crew members was a very attractive flight attendant from Sweden. Her name was Birgitt Nielsen. She was a U.C.L.A. graduate and wanted to pursue a career in costume design for the motion picture/TV industry, and I believe she did.

We engaged in conversation while standing in line for the hotel's feature movie presentation, <u>Crack in the World</u>, with Dana Andrews. This young lady was very easy to talk to and obviously pretty sharp—an enjoyable person. I was married and she didn't seem to be interested in anything along serious lines. We had dinner together on a couple occasions and went to see <u>Sound of Music</u> starring Julie Andrews at one of Tokyo's movie theaters. And then there was the rickshaw ride in Hibiya Park—my idea.

I flagged down a rickshaw puller who was somewhat elderly and about five feet tall, but lean and muscular. I requested a ride around the park for Birgitt and me without asking what he was going to charge—cavalier and stupid.

Papasan towed us for about forty-five minutes and it was a beautiful ride. It was my one and only time in a rickshaw. At the conclusion of the ride, I asked how much his fee was. His response was forty-five thousand yen. At that time the exchange rate was three hundred and sixty yen to one American dollar (those days are long gone). So we're talking about roughly one hundred and twenty five dollars. That was more than I was carrying with me. I knew that Tokyo was expensive, but wow!

My first thought was to challenge "Pop" for trying to shake me down for too much money. Then my second thought was, I can see the newspaper story, American pro wrestler assaults elderly Japanese rickshaw puller! I was saved when Birgitt offered to make up the difference to avoid an embarrassing situation—class lady to the rescue!

I guess the lesson to be learned would be: When one purchases a service, one should inquire about the price before one accepts the service. This is also known as common sense.

I saw Birgitt's name as a costume designer in the credits of a network TV show on a few occasions. I hope she did well.

Incident: 1970's, San Diego, California. Sometimes, at social gatherings, people would either recognize me as a professional wrestler or the word would get around that I was in the business. Invariably, the two questions I would be asked were, "Is pro wrestling real?" or "What's your wrestling name?" To the first question my pat answer was for them to take out a license and find out. Actually, I stole that response from Mike Mazurki, Hollywood character actor and part-time pro wrestler. Thanks Mike. To the second question I would indicate Don Savage and hope they had heard of me or maybe not heard of me.

One night at a party, I had probably consumed one beer too many. This lady, whom I didn't know, had been told that I was a professional wrestler and she approached me asking question number two (my wrestling name). To this day I don't know what induced me to answer, "Crusher

Bo Peep"—maybe the beer? However, this response seemed to take her by surprise, and it did shut her up. Somewhat confused, she turned around and walked away from me. Score one for C. Bo Peep! I used this technique on some other occasions, and it seemed to work.

Over a five-year period, I purchased several N.F.L. jerseys and on a few of them, the personalization on the back was C. Bo Peep. The others had Savage and they all carried my service football number, fifty-two.

Sometimes when I'm wearing one of my Bo Peep jerseys, someone will ask me if my name is really Bo Peep. My answer is that Bo Peep is Ukrainian. The double "e" is pronounced as long "a" and the final "p" is silent—Bo Pay. So far no one has ever questioned that response. I think if you give information in an authoritative manner, people tend to believe it.

Incident: 1960's, San Diego, California. There was a male wrestling spectator in San Diego who just completely disliked me. Even when I was a babyface, he hated me. He attended matches at the Coliseum and the Sports Arena and there must have been something about me that he simply could not tolerate. When I was working as a heel—okay, but when I was a babyface, I couldn't figure it out.

This guy would scream that I was a terrible person who didn't deserve to be in sports. He knew that I was a teacher and coach and he constantly reminded me that I was a disgrace to education and my California teaching credential should be revoked.

After listening to his relentless verbal attacks for too long, I had finally had it with this jerk. I had finished working and was watching one of the other matches. Big Mouth approached me and started in again. This time I told him to shut up for a minute and listen to what I had to say. He did. He wasn't drunk and he seemed to be paying attention. What a surprise! I informed him that Russ Savage was not only my principal at El Capitan, but was also my dad. Big mouth had made comments about how my principal should know what a "turd" I was and how I was such a bad example for young people. Well, I was going to give him a chance to express his sentiments to Russ.

I told the fan to wait just a moment, went back to the dressing room, wrote down the school's phone number and presented it to him. I advised him to call Russ if he had the fortitude to do so. I assumed that Big Mouth was all talk and this would be the end of it. Yeah, sure . . .

The next day at school, a student delivered a message to my classroom. It was from Russ, "My office at lunch." I had put Big Mouth out of my mind and didn't make an association until I entered Russ' office. He was seated behind his desk and didn't appear to be too happy. Russ knew I was in the wrestling business and had even covered one of my afternoon classes on occasion so that I could make a flight to a booking. He indicated that he had received a phone call that morning from a complete cuckoo who was blabbering about Don Savage and how Savage was a discredit to education and shouldn't be teaching or coaching young people.

Russ did his best to keep a straight face but half way through the reprimand, he totally cracked up and lost his focus. We both laughed and I related the story behind Big Mouth. I believe Russ was amazed that I had to deal with such characters. He asked me to please not involve him in my pro wrestling world in the future. Once was enough!

Incident: Late 1960's, Los Angeles, California. I don't know whose idea this was but the office decided to have the Olympic Auditorium host a "Frat Night," inviting all the

Los Angeles area college fraternities for one dollar per person admission and half price on the concessions (including beer). This was going to spell disaster. The Olympic could seat around ten thousand people and that night there must have been at least six thousand college kids in attendance.

During the first match, things began to get rowdy and conditions didn't improve. The evening's card called for six matches with the main event billed as a sixteen man battle royal.

By the time the main event participants entered the ring, the place was already out of control. I was scheduled to be the twelfth wrestler eliminated, so I knew I was going to be working for a while.

The Olympic was going through an interior renovation, and plastic covers had been placed on the backs of the spectator seats. Some idiot removed a cover and promptly hurled it in the direction of the ring. Other folks followed and immediately we wrestlers were in the midst of a barrage of plastic seat covers. This wasn't life threatening but capable of possible minor injury.

I picked the biggest thing I could find to hide behind, Gorilla Monsoon, who was about six feet five and close to three hundred pounds. Gino and I waltzed around the ring that was now covered with seat covers, and I could hear him laughing and calling me a coward. At one time I peeked out and saw our security officer, an off duty Los Angeles police lieutenant, being suspended by his necktie in the middle of a bunch of frat boys.

Sirens—a riot had been declared and the L.A.P.D. was arriving to defuse the chaos. We battle royal wrestlers were escorted from the ring without finishing our match and the college kids didn't care. They just wanted to party and raise hell.

When I departed the Olympic, there were still about twenty police cruisers in the parking lot and it seemed that order had been pretty well restored. I hope someone learned from this. College kids and too much available beer are not a good mixture.

Incident: 1960, Hampton, Virginia. I had worked the semi-main event in a match with Alex Medina. During the intermission, our referee became ill and couldn't continue. The local promoter recruited me to officiate the main event—a women's tag team match. Two of the ladies, Mary Jane Mull and Jackie Wilson, I knew because they had been in the territory for a while. Their opponents were from up north and I wasn't acquainted with them.

Mary Jane and Jackie were good gals but they couldn't resist a "rib." I was going to be the target of that "rib." They knew that I had brought my wife, Dorothy, with me to the show and were bound to provide me with about thirty minutes of pure embarrassment.

I refereed their match wearing my boots, tights, and a t-shirt so it was difficult to hide the blushing redness that I would exhibit for most of the bout. When those ladies didn't have their hands where <u>they</u> didn't belong, they had my hands where <u>they</u> didn't belong. One time they caught me in the middle of a four wrestler "scrum" (pile) and I could hear them all laughing. Jackie asked me, "I wonder what Dorothy thinks about this?" as she promptly placed my right hand on her left boob.

The finish couldn't have come soon enough, and when it did, I was the first one to leave the ring. I received a rousing round of applause from the audience. I believe they were somewhat sympathetic for what I had just endured—close to total humiliation.

The only reference Dorothy made to that night's activities was asking me if I had fun. She knew I had been set up.

The professional wrestling business, like other areas of the entertainment industry, can provide some rather unique experiences; some comical, some strange, but all different to a degree.

CHAPTER 19

Injuries: I've Had a Few

Let's take an anatomical inventory from top to bottom:

Head:	three brain concussions
Neck:	no fractures, several sprains
Shoulder:	damaged rotator cuff
Chest:	contusions
Back:	spinal arthritis and spinal stenosis
Hip:	replacement (1994) and revision (2002)
Knee:	two sprains
Ankle:	sprains
Right elbow:	stiffness and soreness
Wrist:	simple fracture

Not all of these injuries were related to the wrestling business. Some were due to ten years of football. Can you imagine the number of times, as an offensive lineman, I attacked a seven man blocking sled, blocking dummies, and light bags over ten years? This number doesn't even take into consideration live contact—games, drills, and scrimmages against defensive personnel who didn't have my best interests at heart. I'm sure these collisions didn't do my lower back a whole lot of good. Don't misunderstand me;

I firmly believe that football is a great game, but on me, it took its toll.

My first brain concussion occurred in high school. I was executing a downfield block and caught the defensive back's knee to my head. I dreamed I could see a couple in the stands, and the man was commenting to the woman about the shot I had taken. I made it off the field on my own and then collapsed on the sideline. I spent one night in the hospital.

The second concussion took place in college where I had to play some defense. I was rushing the passer and had to go through a back protecting the quarterback. He must have delivered an elbow to my chin. Although I continued to play, I didn't remember a thing until I became aware at halftime in the dressing room.

I sustained my third concussion in pro wrestling. I had been "married" to Pedro Morales for a week, working essentially the same match in different cities. We had used a finish where Pedro would come off the top rope planting his butt on my chest followed by a cover to end the match. This was routine for five nights. The sixth night was a big house show at L.A.'s Olympic Auditorium. To this day I don't know what went wrong, but my head made really hard contact with the mat in an unforgiving ring—lights out! Evidently, they placed me on a stretcher and transported me to the dressing room. On the way up the aisle I must have come to. Victor, the Wrestling Bear, was right beside me being led to the ring to work with The Destroyer. I remember reaching out and petting Victor, and then it was "goodnight" again. I came around in the shower with the athletic commission physician checking to see how I was. I guess I was okay because I drove back to San Diego that night with no apparent problem. It's a good thing I have a hard head.

While we're covering head injuries, we might as well mention the cauliflower ear syndrome. My left ear damage is minor compared to some ears in the business. A "tin" ear or ears was sort of a badge of combat worn proudly by many of the boys in wrestling.

A cauliflower ear develops when there is bruising to the ear tissue. If this bruising is not medically attended to in a short period of time, the aggravated fluid hardens and becomes essentially gristle with a permanent deformity. Side headlocks were the usual cause of the condition and headlocks were a primary hold in pro wrestling.

I sustained my first "tin ear" in 1959 while I was with the V.W.A. I was in the Navy and saw a Navy physician. After a brief examination he informed me that unless I was going to stop wrestling, it didn't make much sense to treat the problem because it would occur again and again over time—end of discussion.

My neck injuries were minimal. In football, we aimed with our heads and blocked and tackled with our shoulders. In addition, in the weight room, I spent a lot of time working on my neck and shoulder muscles. In wrestling, most of my neck damage came from taking head on bumps into corner turnbuckle pads improperly—bad angle or impact, usually my own fault.

The rotator cuff problem was due to my mishandling of free weights during a bench press exercise. Once again, it was a mistake on my part. That injury bothers me now more than it did during my athletic years. I'm sure age has something to do with it.

Chest bruising was not uncommon in the business. Forearm smashes and Judo chops were the primary causes.

When we were hot and sweaty, we didn't feel these shots to the chest, and they were much preferred over a punch in the mouth. A heavily laid in forearm or chop sounded great to the fans and other than occasional bruising, didn't create lasting damage.

My back problems are the result of both football and wrestling exposure. Also running or jogging on pavement is not a good idea. Constant impact and trauma over distance and time take its measure.

I have a ton of osteoarthritis in my lower back and spinal stenosis which causes impaired motor operation in my legs hampering my ability to walk smoothly. Too many hard bumps in too many hard rings over too many years can cause some real damage to the human body, but when we are young and invulnerable, we don't really take this into consideration. With age, sometimes comes wisdom—very slowly.

Probably ninety percent of the wrestlers who spent years in the business have had either one or both hips replaced. Usually the left hip is the first to go because maneuvers are based on left side orientation—left side headlocks, left leg holds, left arm or wrist locks, left arm drags, etc. The left hip takes most of the impact and punishment. Sometime watch wrestling on TV—everything operates from the left. The reason for this is to minimize tactical confusion in the ring. Even the tie-up technique is left hand on the opponent's neck. However, in Mexico, all maneuvers were from the right side—go figure. Anytime I worked with a Mexican wrestler who was new to the territory, part of the game plan was to make sure he was aware of left side protocol. If we weren't on the same frequency, real problems could occur.

I underwent a hip replacement in 1994. The procedure went well and recovery was fairly rapid with physical therapy and a positive attitude helping greatly. The three possible problems after a hip replacement are lower component dislodging, upper component dislocating, and infection. Well, I batted two out of three. A staph infection settled in the tissue around the upper component and it caused a multitude of problems. In 2002 a revision was performed in which the upper component was removed and replaced, and this provided a temporary resolve. Staph is stubborn and more flare-ups occurred. A staph infection isn't cured; it's controlled with antibiotics—heavy duty antibiotics. And that's where I am now—we'll see.

Fortunately, my knee injuries have been relatively minor. In football I sustained sprains, and jogging on pavement caused fluid on the knee twice. This required draining and the injection of Cortisone to reduce inflammation and discomfort.

I experienced only one knee problem while wrestling as a pro. In 1971, while I was in Japan, the Los Angeles office renovated the ring platform at the Olympic Auditorium transforming it from a boxing slab to a very forgiving wrestling ring. It was about time!

I was working with Rocky Johnson and made an errant pivot on the new surface—ouch! Another minor sprain. Rocky carried me through the rest of the match. It was a kind of bad-good situation with a knee boo-boo, but a very decent ring at the Olympic.

I was hampered by two ankle sprains; one wrestling in college in 1954 and the other playing service football in 1960. Neither injury was considered serious and didn't slow me down a whole lot other than requiring taping for a while.

My right elbow refuses to straighten out completely. The short arm drag, which opens a lot of matches, is the culprit. Remember, all the techniques are left side oriented, so the right arm takes a real impact beating on the mat. After years of punishment, the right elbow has a tendency to lock up, and mine is proof. Once again, the hard ring platforms can be held responsible for this problem.

I fractured my left wrist in high school football. As a part of my rehabilitation therapy, I had to shoot a basketball left handed. To this day I still shoot from the left side—not that I play that much basketball in my seventies.

One of my favorite bumps was being launched over the top rope and rotating my body so that I would land flat on my back on the arena floor, which was wood or concrete with no padding. The "splatting" sound would draw "oooh's and aaah's" from the fans. I protected my head but my back absorbed a pounding. One time, when I was in my thirties and took that bump, I briefly thought about the results this might spell out down the line, and now I know—not good.

Injuries are a part of collision sports. Considering all the impacts I've sustained in one way or another over some thirty years, maybe I could be a lot worse off.

CHAPTER 20

Personalities

Chapter twenty is somewhat lengthy. As a reader, I don't enjoy long chapters. The upside is that you can break this chapter up as you wish.

In my twenty years in the pro wrestling business, I encountered many different people from many different walks of life. I would like to tell you about some of these folks and how they were a part of my experience. I am not presenting these individuals in any particular order because they all played a specific role in one way or another. I'm pretty certain you will recognize some of these names.

Charles Iwamoto (Mr. Moto): Charlie Moto was one of my bosses for most of the time I worked out of the Los Angeles wrestling office. He was a top star in the forties, fifties, sixties, and the first part of the seventies. Charlie was famous as a Japanese villain with his traditional pre-match salt ceremony, sumo warm-up stomps, as well as his Judo and Karate chops, and, of course, his match finishing Japanese sleeper hold. He always wanted his matches to appear as realistic as possible, which was one of the things he impressed upon me—concentrate on one part of the body (arm, leg, back, etc.) and attack it constantly to pursue victory.

Charlie was gruff on the outside but on the inside, he possessed a big heart. He was very good to me, knowing that I was a struggling teacher and coach, and he booked me as much as he could.

Two situations involving Charlie Moto will remain in my memory banks forever. The first incident displayed his family side, although he never talked much about his family, at least not to me.

The L.A. office was running a show at the San Diego Sports Arena and I wasn't scheduled to appear on the card. That night Dorothy was attending a class so I had the duty with the kids who were seven, five, and three years old. Dorothy had gone to her class and at seven p.m. the phone rang. It was Charlie and he indicated that I was needed a.s.a.p. I told him about the kids and his response was, "Bring them, I'll watch them," and he wouldn't take no for an answer. I put on my gear and warm-ups, got the kids into their pajamas and robes, jumped into the car, and set out for the Sports Arena.

We entered the Sports Arena through the truck gate where Charlie was to meet us. As we hustled down the ramp, our son Bill, asked me if this was where they brought in the elephants when the circus was here. I don't know why I remember this. Maybe I was impressed with his observation skills at seven years of age.

Charlie met us at the gate, introduced himself to Bill, Patti, and Karen, and sent me to the dressing room—situation in hand with the kids appearing to be very much at ease.

I was in a tag team match early on the card and when I wasn't in the ring working, I would sneak a glance to see how the kids were doing. From what I could see, Karen was sitting on Charlie's lap and Bill and Patti on each side, and all of them were munching on something. Everyone happy.

Charlie had held up his end of the deal and the children seemed to have had a good time. We arrived home before Dorothy got there. I swore the kids to secrecy and put them in bed. The secrecy part lasted about one day, but thankfully I didn't get into a whole lot of trouble with my wife. Meet the villainous Mr. Moto, the babysitter. Thanks Charlie.

The other humorous Mr. Moto situation occurred in the sixties as well. Charlie was great at selling on his feet or on the mat, but he absolutely refused to be lifted off his feet, which ruled out body slams, back drops, suplexes, etc. An airplane spin was totally out of the question. Any attempt to elevate Charlie met with his automatically weighing one thousand pounds—impossible to lift and that's the way it was! I know because I tried on a few occasions, without success.

The wrestling office sent Charlie and me to Utah to do a studio TV show in Salt Lake City. On our flight from LAX, Charlie fell asleep when we started to taxi out and remained asleep until we arrived at the gate in Salt Lake—great travel companion!

In a tag event, Pepper Gomez and I were matched against Charlie and Harold Sakata (Odd Job in the James Bond film <u>Goldfinger</u>) who was working as either Tosh Togo or The Great Togo; I can't remember. Harold and I had worked together before and had good matches, so when I mentioned my plan to him, he was very willing to participate. He couldn't resist a good "rib," especially if it was on Charlie. We let Pepper in on it and smartened up the referee. Charlie had no idea what was in store for him. This was my opportunity to be devious, which was unusual for me.

The scenario was the following: Pepper and I took over on Harold, "belaboring" him so that he became completely "disoriented." Harold managed to get free and make it to the corner where Charlie was waiting to tag in. As soon as Charlie entered the ring, Harold, still "disoriented," scooped him up and body slammed him right there in their corner. Charlie was caught totally off guard but he sold the bump beautifully and then threatened Harold, creating a great high spot—two outstanding pros at work!

For the remainder of the match, anytime Charlie and I were working together, he called me every name in the book knowing that I had engineered the plot to get him "up in the air." Charlie must have cooled off by the time we flew back to Los Angeles because he went back into his sleep mode.

These two memories of Mr. Moto still bring a smile to my face—Charlie the "nanny" and "Air Charlie."

Art "Boom Boom" Michalik: I met Art in the mid-sixties when we both worked out of the L.A. office. We worked together several times and because we had football in common, got to be friends. The first two times we worked, we got blood the hard way—my nose, when I mistimed an arm drag catching his elbow flush in the face. The second time I launched Art into the corner and intended to follow with a tackle. As I went in, he came out planting his dental bridge into my upper chin. The bridge flew out, and as Art was diving to the mat to cover his teeth, he told me to cover him. That was the only time I every beat Art Michalik. I still sport the scar on my chin from Boom Boom's bridge.

Art Michalik earned his college degree at St. Ambrose in Davenport, Iowa. He evidently played some pretty decent football and was either drafted by or signed as a free agent with the San Francisco Forty-Niners where he became defensive standout. For those of you who go back a long way, Art was responsible for lacerating Cleveland Brown's star quarterback Otto Graham's face, requiring several stitches at half-time. Art indicates that Otto was somewhat gracious about the incident, however, his offensive line wasn't quite as forgiving and attempted to destroy him during the entire second half of the game.

Art played a few seasons with the Forty-Niner's and then was traded to Pittsburgh. While he was with the Steelers, injuries slowed him down and guided him out of football into pro wrestling, working from the Chicago office.

When I met Art, he had re-located to Los Angeles and was going through a divorce. With football in common, we sometimes traveled to bookings together, sharing experiences and stories.

I hope I was at least a tad bit instrumental in encouraging Art to acquire his California teaching credential so that he could teach and coach in high school—which he did. Art became a very successful football coach in Orange County, California at a couple of schools.

As a side note, Art married his second wife, Bev, who was the bus driver responsible for transporting his athletic teams. As of our last contact, Art and Bev were doing fine living in Orange County.

Johnny Kace: John Kakacek and I were in Japan together in 1965. He had a degree from Marquette University and was working in as well as being booked out of the Chicago office.

Johnny and I hit it off immediately. We were both married with kids and had a lot in common. He had thought about entering education but hadn't really pursued it. Down the line he attained his credential, taught, and finally retired as a District Superintendent in Antioch, Illinois.

John had a great sense of humor and when he chose to, he could furnish a perfect impersonation of the film great,

W.C. Fields, in both appearance and voice. He was a dead ringer. The Hotel New Otani had seventeen floors including a rotating cocktail lounge and restaurant on the top floor. It featured a three hundred and sixty degree view of Tokyo in one hour's time—spectacular! The elevators in the hotel were manned by lovely young ladies as attendants and John would invariably, in his W.C. mode, request the eighteenth floor by saying, "Number eighteen, my little chickadee." This totally confused the poor kids until he broke down and told them he was kidding. W. C. Kakacek was always good for a laugh.

On the downside, Johnny had a totally foul mouth just through habit. It wasn't in anger; it was just the way he communicated. I'm sure this was corrected when he entered education—I hope!

On one occasion the Japanese press treated Paul Diamond, John, and me to lunch in downtown Tokyo. Paul had something to attend to after our meal, so John and I took a walk through the Ginza shopping area which had shops displaying all kinds of merchandise. Johnny caught my attention pointing to one of the stores and said, "Hey Don, look at this quaint little gift shop." All of a sudden I'm thinking that John verbalized a complete thought without any profanity or vulgarity. I was in shock. Then he followed up with, "Goddamn, they've got a ton of fuckin' shit in there!" Oh well, back to the norm.

Johnny was a great worker. He possessed poise, timing, and style. One time he was working with Giant Baba (seven feet tall and three hundred pounds). John was five feet nine inches tall and about two hundred forty pounds and although John was doing a job, it was so convincing, it appeared as if he were going to defeat Baba up until the finish of the match. Johnny had a tremendous work ethic.

He was making good money in Japan and he wanted to earn his money. I'm sure he took the same model into education.

John knew how to have fun, and he also knew when it was time to work hard. He was a quality guy.

Freddie Blassie: Freddie, like Ric Flair, was the total professional wrestling package. He was completely dedicated to the business. Every time I worked with Freddie, I learned something. Whether it be in the ring, laying out the mechanics of a match, or interviewing, his skills were top grade. He was always very emphatic about how a match should go, and if someone didn't measure up to his expectation, he would let that someone know about it.

One time I was interviewing on TV in San Diego and my end of the interview was "dying." Freddie saw what was occurring and he jumped in to save the spot, making a good situation out of a bad one. The business was his primary concern.

Fred always said what was on his mind. Freddie, Jack Garfono, and I were sharing a dressing room at the Olympic Auditorium for a TV taping show one night. Jack was serving as an assistant football coach at one of L.A.'s Catholic high schools—a football powerhouse. He was relating to me a situation that occurred during that school's Los Angeles Section Championship game at the L.A. Coliseum. Blassie was nearby and listening to our conversation. It seems that Jack's team was trailing by five points very late in the game. With only seconds remaining and a fourth and goal situation, Jack's team ran an out of the backfield circle pass pattern. The kid was by himself in the end zone and dropped a perfect pass. It was game over—loss! Of course the kid felt terrible after the game and was in tears. Jack tried to console him saying, "Hey, this happens to the best players in football." Blassie was taking all this in and offered his version of what he would have said to the kid. "You Goddamn, motherfucking, butter fingered son-of-a-bitch, you probably lost me my fucking job!" Good old Freddie was just flowing over with empathy and sympathy. I don't think Fred was really serious in his comment. I believe he was just trying to lighten up the moment.

Classy Freddie Blassie was one of a kind and a true professional wrestler, a credit to the business.

George "The Animal" Steele: What can I say? George and I were in Japan together in 1971. I always enjoyed observing George whenever he was in the spotlight. He was a show all by himself, standing about six feet two inches tall, weighing a good two hundred eighty pounds, covered with matted body hair with the exception of his massive shaved head. He reminded me of Thor Johnson who played creepy character roles in several horror films in the 1940's and 1950s. During his matches, George always managed to wander out in the audience scaring the crap out of Japanese ladies and kids. George never hurt anyone but his presence alone created havoc with the folks in attendance.

George was a high school industrial arts teacher and wrestling coach in Ohio and also moonlighted in the business for Bruno San Martino out of Pittsburgh. His wrestling career really took off when Vince McMahon's W.W.F. organization programmed him on top in the 1980's and 1990's.

During the 1971 "tour from hell" in Japan, George and I were tag team partners in Osaka. It was our second to last remaining booking with one TV show in Tokyo and then home to the United States, and we were ready to come home. The schedule for us, in Osaka, was to be transported by taxi to the arena (in our warm-ups), work our match, and then taxied back to our hotel.

When George and I arrived at the hotel, we went straight to the bar, warm-ups, sweaty bodies, and all. We ordered about three beers apiece and powered those down in a hurry. The bar was air-conditioned and it was pretty cool in that room, which really felt good. As George sat at the bar, his perspiration began to form wispy clouds of steam that rose from his shaved head. This fascinated the bar patrons and they gathered around us to observe this strange phenomenon. George loved it! He was enjoying his beer and still entertaining people.

Also while we were at the bar, George and I were raving about a woman vocalist on the lounge's TV, insisting that she was one of the loveliest and most talented ladies we had ever seen. Everyone around us laughed. The bartender, who spoke English, informed us that our "heart-throb" was, in reality, a female impersonator. So much for love at first sight.

George loved the business and thoroughly enjoyed carrying out his ring persona of a demented, strange "animal."

"Jarrin" John Cable: In 1960 our service football schedule took us to Florida to play two semi-professional teams; one in Ft. Lauderdale and the other in Key West. I don't remember a whole lot about the Ft. Lauderdale game except that we won twenty two to zero and, because we stayed in a motel, we had to find separate lodging for our black athletes. Segregation was still in force. The day after our Ft. Lauderdale game, Sunday, we departed by bus for Key West where we would be lodged at the Naval Receiving Station and not have to put up with the racial discrimination bullshit.

In downtown Key West, we soon located the Rainbow Room Cocktail Lounge which would become our watering hole for that week. It was in short walking distance and the employees treated us exceptionally well. It was our home away from home, so to speak.

The Key West media quickly picked up on the angle that I was a professional wrestler and playing opposite me would be "Jarrin" John Cable, all six feet one and three hundred pounds of him. For the media, this was a match up made in heaven—pro wrestler versus three hundred pound giant. It received newspaper print and even a television interview featuring John and me—some great hype!

Semi-pro football was big in South Florida and there was a significant amount of betting associated with it. The Key West Jaguars were undefeated and untied after six games and were picked as heavy favorites over us. As it turned out, we were going to cost some bettors a few bucks.

We won the coin toss and chose to receive the opening kick-off which we returned to our own twenty-six yard line—first and ten. When our offense lined up over the ball, Cable set himself in the strong side gap (tight end side). When I snapped the ball, "Jarrin" John slanted to the outside and stopped an off tackle run. On the second play, he did the same thing and once again messed up the play. The third play resulted in much the same. He didn't make the tackle but he disrupted the line of scrimmage so that a teammate made the hit. Although John was pretty heavy, he possessed good foot speed and could play football, and because he was stunting away from me, there was no way I could block him or even get to him. We punted, and while our defense was on the field, "Tuffy" Parsons, our offensive line coach, and I put our heads together to solve the problem. The solution was a short inside trap—take John the way he wanted to go.

The Key West offense couldn't move the ball, and after their punt, we took possession on our own twenty-two. John lined up in that same strong side gap and, on the snap, we executed what appeared to be a perfect trap play—seventy-eight yards and six points. I caught Cable in the middle of his slant or loop, and away we went. That early game play was the turning point. After that, it was all over for the Key West Jaguars and a sixty-two to zero win for the Norfolk Navy Tars. We scored at will and stopped them cold. It was one of our best team efforts of the season. With the score forty-two to zero at halftime, the first unit offense was pulled and we enjoyed the game from the sideline. After the game, John and I met and shook hands. It's easy to be a gracious winner but not that much fun being "blown out." However, John was very gracious and we both agreed that it was just one of those nights—it happens.

It seems that the owner of our watering hole, The Rainbow Room, had won a ton of wagering money. When we showed up after the game, the bar was lined with bottles of champagne and drinks were on the house for team members as well as coaching and support staff. "Jarrin" John Cable and his lovely wife joined us and it was a pretty good after-game party enjoyed by all—well, almost all.

Bo Bo Brazil: Bo stood a good six feet five inches tall and weighed in at three hundred pounds. He was an African-American athlete who was in a class all by himself—a great worker with a super light touch, and he made the business look real with him famous cocoa head butt that brought audiences to their feet. He was the epitome of a superstar babyface.

I had the pleasure of working with and teaming with Bo on a number of occasions. He must have liked me because whenever we were together, Bo made me look good. Bo Bo Brazil was always up for a rib and I happened to be one of his targets. We had just finished a tag match for Wednesday night TV at the Olympic Auditorium. Bo and I were in the same dressing room with a couple of the other boys. I always made it a habit to brush my teeth before I showered. I was brushing away over a sink with my eyes closed, oblivious to everything around me. When I opened my eyes, I observed a huge black penis just lying in the basin. Totally surprised, I quickly lifted my head to see Bo with that grin, which shortly turned into one of his belly laughs. He then advised me that it might be a good idea to use mouthwash instead of brushing, which I did for the remainder of my wrestling career.

On another occasion, Bo and I were working a single match in Bakersfield, California. It was going to be a quick job with Bo going over. We opened with my hitting the ropes and launching a tackle into Bo, who stood his ground as I bounced off him and took a bump. On my attempted second tackle, as I hurled myself into the ropes, the cable must have parted and I was on an express trip to the second or third row of spectators (I wasn't counting). Fortunately no one, including me, was injured. I climbed back into the ring and we finished. I remember as I attacked that top rope, Bo's eyes grew as big as saucers. His post-match comment was, "The last thing I saw was the soles of Savage's boots going up, up, and away!"

Bo Bo Brazil was a pleasure to be around and was admired and respected by his peers in the wrestling business.

Roy Shire: Roy Shire was probably one of professional wrestling's best businessmen. He promoted the San Francisco

Bay Area but extended his territory from Sacramento to Fresno. Before promoting, he worked for years as one of the Shire Brothers tag combo along with, I believe, Ray Stevens, and they did very well all around the country as a notorious heel team.

When Roy began promoting, he would meet with wrestlers who were new to his territory and let them know up front that he wasn't paying people to lie around on their butts. He insisted on action, high spots, and realistic matches. Roy paid well and always had top caliber talent working for him.

A couple of things I learned from Roy were: (1) If you're a babyface in a tag match, you never make your own comeback on the heels. You manage to tag your partner and let him make the comeback, which makes more sense. (2) If you've been "mauled" by the heel or heels and thrown out of the ring, struggle back in over the bottom rope—remember you should be "hurting." Once again this just reflects common sense.

Roy was present at every show I worked for him whether it was a house show or TV studio show. He wanted to be on top of everything that was going on. As I was nearing the end of my wrestling career, I asked him one night about his retirement plans. Roy answered with a completely straight face, "When I can't think of anymore finishes for matches, I'll consider retiring." I believe he meant it. Roy Shire was a super promoter!

Howard Ferguson: Howard had played football at Southern Illinois University before joining our 1959-1960 Navy team at Norfolk. He was an offensive guard and defensive noseman and probably the reason I had pretty good success in service football. As a center, I had to go against him every day. Howard was five feet ten inches tall and weighed about two hundred twenty pounds, had great agility, and he could smell a football. When we scrimmaged, if I could block him fifty percent of the time, I'd call it a good day. After working against Ferguson, the opposing nosemen I had to take on seemed pretty routine. Howard was awesome and I learned a lot from him.

Howard Ferguson, who was black, was an "informal civil rights activist" and constantly spoke for racial equality. Every once in a while he would get on his anti-discrimination soap box in the locker room and the white guys would jokingly get on him, indicating that if he didn't knock it off, there would be white sheets burning crosses at his house that night. Howie would always reply, "If those sheets are there tonight—no problem, but if they're there tomorrow night—problem, because I would have shot them on their first appearance and on the second night they would be ghosts and I'm scared of ghosts!"

It was common knowledge that Howard packed a gun when we played ball in the deep South. His rational was, "They might get me, but I'll get six of them and maybe twelve if I get a chance to re-load." Fortunately, as far as I know, there was never a situation that might have forced his hand, which was fine with me.

I never had contact with Howard Ferguson after our service football days. I hope he did well back in Illinois.

Super Star Billy Graham: My first contact with Billy Graham was in the mid-sixties in Los Angeles. He had teamed up with Dr. Jerry Graham with whom I had worked back in my V.W.A. time on the East Coast. Jerry had gained a hundred pounds but was still a great worker. Billy was not. Lou Anthony and I were doing a job for the Grahams in a TV tag match at the Olympic Auditorium. If it wasn't Billy's first match, it was close. He was terrible, screwing up every high spot and the finish. It was a long fifteen minutes and Lou, Jerry, and I earned our money just covering for Billy's mistakes. After the match, Jerry spent a good half-hour lecturing Billy on his sub-par performance and Billy simply nodded in agreement. I know he felt terrible.

The next time I worked with Billy was in the early seventies—what a difference! We were in a single match, and he had come a long way toward becoming an accomplished worker. I don't know who had coached Billy, but whoever it was had done one heck of a job. Timing, technique, and working the house—it was all there. It was a pleasure working with him and we had a great match.

Billy went straight to the top. He spent a great amount of time in Vince McMahon's W.W.F. company as one of Vince's strong heels. Unfortunately, Billy developed a steroid body and it caught up with him. He collaborated on an article dealing with the downside of steroid use and indicated that it had essentially destroyed him physically. I framed that article and hung it on my classroom wall and in my office when I was a counselor.

Billy Graham was a true superstar but it's difficult to maintain that status when the hip, knee, and ankle joints are gone— a sad ending to a fine career.

Richard "Dick the Bruiser" Afflis: The first time I worked with Dick was on Wednesday night TV at the Olympic in L.A. He was six feet tall and a good two hundred sixty pounds and not a lot of excess weight. He was pretty solid. His personal demeanor was so different from his ring persona, which was loud, mean, and "I can destroy anybody at any time." Out of the spotlight, he was quiet and all business, constantly checking his booking schedule.

Jules Strongbow introduced me to Dick and the first thing I noticed was his handshake. In the wrestling business the boys always offered the "limp fish" grip when we shook hands. This signified that we knew the business was work, and we were "loose" in the ring. I don't know how that got started but it was standard operating procedure for some reason. When I offered the "limp fish" shake to Dick, his shake was firm and he chuckled and said very quietly, "You're either the loosest S.O.B. in the business or a fucking queer." So much for the "loose" handshake. I never used that technique again. I could demonstrate how loose I was in the ring where it counted.

Dick Afflis was a master at what he did. If a carpenter sold properly for Dick, he could make a match look frighteningly realistic and he was so easy to work with. He'd telegraph his punches with a thumb to where the next blow was going to land, which made my job easier. His finish was a flying knee drop off the top rope, and his only admonition was for me to keep my arms and hands flat on the mat cover, away from my throat, which was the point of impact—there was no impact. As devastating as the move looked, Dick made no contact with me. All I had to do was sell, sell, sell!

Richard Afflis must have like me because in the half-dozen times we worked together, he always gave me at least one comeback or high spot to make me look good. Dick the Bruiser was one of the greats!

John "Skull" Murphy: I worked with "Skull" Murphy only once; a TV job at the Olympic. This match was a "blood bath" that was featured in John Greensmith's October, 1969, Inside Wrestling magazine article about me, Don Savage, school teacher, and pro wrestler. Unfortunately, the blood was all mine, but we got it the easy way.

John needed a ride to the airport, which was essentially on my way back to San Diego, so I volunteered transportation.

It was about a thirty minute ride and we had time to talk. John was a Canadian, and we shared information about similarities and differences in our two countries with regard to family, education, opportunities, and other things. It was a very pleasant conversation in which we discussed some of the basic values dealing with living life.

I was truly shocked to hear of John's passing in 1970 which was apparently a suicide. I guess I didn't "read" John that well during our brief encounter in the late sixties. Something in his life must have gone terribly wrong. He was a success at what he did—pro wrestling as one of the top names in the business. Who knows?

In my English classes I taught a poem titled "Richard Cory" by Edwin Robinson. The selection was about a gentleman, Richard Cory, who appeared to have it all. He had attained wealth, was highly admired and respected by his peers, and quite popular with the ladies. In spite of all this, one night, he put a bullet through his head. I guess, sometimes what we see on the outside of a person is not what's going on inside. Maybe this was John "Skull" Murphy.

Chuey and Carollo: Here come the Rams! Don Chuey, out of the University of North Carolina, and Joe Carollo, from the University of Notre Dame, played guard and tackle in the Los Angeles Rams' offensive line. In the off-season, they chose to pursue professional wrestling as a second career. When I first met them, we talked football a lot. It seems that George Allen had been hired as the Rams new head coach, replacing Harland Svare. This made Chuey and Carollo ecstatic because Svare had required his athletes to complete training camp mile runs with specific times according to their playing positions. Don and Joe hated this with a passion. George Allen did not believe in the qualifying run which made most of the Rams team members quite happy.

Chuey and Carollo were classic examples that the transition from pro football to pro wrestling was not always easy. They just couldn't get some of their football instincts out of their mindset. One example of this was their execution of mid-ring tackles. The protocol calls for the tackler to make contact and then move at a right angle to the ropes for the next tackle or whatever is scheduled to follow. This way the recipient of the tackle knows the direction from which the next move is coming—simple, right? Not for Chuey and Carollo because they insisted on tackling and continuing right on over the tackle recipient reflecting their football mentality. Another example was their working punches, which were terrible. The office talked them into throwing forearms instead of punches which was great for Don and Joe because they did that all the time in their football contact—problem solved to a degree.

The first time I worked with them in a tag match, they had just changed over from punches to forearms and were somewhat tentative in execution. I instructed them to lay those forearms in, which they did at my expense. These were big strong guys who, at that time, were having trouble differentiating between the concept of "snug" and "loose." But, they were trying and they did improve.

As far as I know, Chuey and Carollo didn't stay with the business for too long but while they were with us, they provided some good entertainment for the rest of the boys.

Mike Mazurki: Mike Mazurki was an accomplished character actor who had a multitude of film roles during his years in show business. He was extremely versatile and could portray bad guys, good guys, or whatever was needed. He was a real talent. Mike was a graduate of Manhattan

College in New York City. He was an outstanding athlete and after college, ventured into acting and professional wrestling with great success in both areas.

I didn't personally meet Mike until the late sixties. I had worked on a TV wrestling show in Hollywood and was waiting for my check. I heard this husky voice call out, "Hey Giovanni, come over here!" I immediately recognized Mike and joined him for a brief conversation. He gave me some words of advice and encouragement with regard to the wrestling business. It was a well spent few minutes.

Mike was doing some refereeing in the L.A. territory and worked some of my matches. One night I was working in a tag match at either the Los Angeles Sports Arena or the Forum in Inglewood. Our wrestling card had been sandwiched between two ice events and sheets of plywood had been laid on top of the ice. The floor and the building were both pretty chilly.

Mazurki was refereeing our match. The finish called for the heels tossing me out of the ring to the arena floor where I was to lie injured. The heels would then team up on my partner and cover him, winning the match.

As I lay on the cold floor selling my injury, I developed chills and began to shake and shiver. Mike looked over the top rope and observed my situation. A look of panic appeared on his face and he yelled, "Savage, are you having a fit?" I tried to signal him that I was okay but by now, I was the focus of the ringsiders' attention, which prohibited any obvious sign on my part. I don't know if Mike got my signal but we completed the match as scheduled. Afterward we laughed about what had taken place—"the best laid plans of mice and men . . ."

Mike Mazurki and I had hit it off pretty well. He was not only a quality character actor, he was also a quality character.

Don Duffy: In my opinion, Don Duffy was one of the best carpenters in professional wrestling. Even though he was doing a job, he possessed the ability to absolutely convince a wrestling audience that he was on his way to winning a match right up to the finish. Don was a great heel, inducing fans to despise him as soon as he entered the ring. His demeanor expressed contempt for all in attendance and he worked aggressively with tactics that automatically drew a lot of crowd heat. His mechanics and timing were excellent.

Don was employed as a cargo hauler with Flying Tigers Airline based at LAX, so the business was a part-time opportunity for him. He wasn't particularly big (five feet ten inches tall and two hundred pounds) but he was a great worker and showman.

I think Don's only problem was that he wanted to be a star, and that just wasn't in the cards. He would come up with some wild ideas to promote himself to the top and some of them backfired.

One night at Olympic Auditorium TV, Don came up with one of his wildest ideas. He and I were doing a straight falls job in a tag match with Pedro Morales and Louis Hernandez. Don brought a Flying Tigers co-worker with him, and this was the plan: The co-worker was to be our corner assistant ("stooge"—similar to Fritz, the laboratory helper in the film Frankenstein). He was dressed in shabby black attire with a built up shoe on one foot simulating a short leg and definite limp. Of course Don and I were the heels and from the outset, verbally and physically mistreated our assistant, which got some good heat.

After Morales and Hernandez took the first fall, Don and I blamed the stooge for our failure and commenced to take out our anger with punches and kicks on the poor guy. As he was crawling helplessly on all fours to avoid a more severe beating, Pedro and Louis came to the stooge's rescue and covered both Don and me to win the match. What we didn't know was that the stooge's platform shoe must have had a protruding nail, and as he crawled around the ring on all fours, he was destroying a fifteen hundred dollar mat cover. Promoter Jules Strongbow was taking all this in and just bowed and shook his head in disbelief—another Duffy idea gone bad.

I don't know how long Don Duffy remained with the business but while he was in it, he made quite an impact—sometimes good, sometimes not so good.

Dick Lane and Jimmy Lennon: Dick Lane and Jimmy Lennon were voices of TV Wrestling in Los Angeles during my time in the business. Dick was the hold-by-hold commentator and Jimmy was the ring announcer at the Olympic Auditorium. They both were outstanding at what they did.

Dick Lane was an accomplished movie and TV character actor with a ton of roles on his resume. He portrayed comedy, drama, and worked with some of the top names in the film industry. In professional wrestling, his ringside observations truly enhanced the activity taking place inside the ring, and his dressing room interviews with the boys and managers were classic! Dick possessed a great gift for words and expressions, and this talent made him an integral part of the wrestling presentation. He was liked and respected by the wrestlers and management and any ideas he had with regard to stimulating promotion were welcomed.

Dick always had a new joke for me and they were essentially clean jokes. Listening to Dick relate the stories was as much fun as the jokes themselves. One night at the Olympic, Dick came to me with a problem. He was going to conduct a locker room interview with Freddie Blassie and Freddie wanted to punctuate the interview by smashing empty beer cans on his forehead. Dick knew I was a beer drinker and thought it was a waste of beer to pour the can contents down the drain, so . . .

He commissioned me to make sure the cans were empty. Fortunately, Paul Diamond was driving me back to San Diego that night.

Dick Lane's ability to put into words what was going on in the ring and dressing room was a real boon to the business in Southern California.

Jimmy Lennon was the golden voice of center ring at the Olympic Auditorium. He was extremely smooth in his wrestler introductions with his Irish tenor tones projecting throughout the building. I don't think I ever heard him make a mistake in his presentations. Jimmy would always check with me, as I entered the ring, to make sure his information was current. He was always very cordial with me asking how things were in San Diego and how school was going.

Every once in a while Jimmy would wander down to the dressing room to assist Dick Lane with an interview or to just shoot the breeze with the boys, and he always had an Irish joke to share. I don't believe there was an Irish joke he didn't know and he presented them with a totally straight face, as if he were delivering his ring announcements. Jimmy Lennon was fun to be around.

In my opinion, Jimmy's son, Jimmy Lennon, Jr. is a carbon copy of his dad in both appearance and voice. He and Michael Buffer are the best going in the ring announcer department, as far as I'm concerned. They are articulate, informed, and bring class to their specialty providing a real contribution to any ring event.

Thank you, Dick Lane and Jimmy Lennon, for making my time in the wrestling business more enjoyable.

I guess part of most any lifetime experience is getting to know and deal with people. The folks I've mentioned in chapter twenty essentially played some role with regard to a lesson to be learned or an idea to be examined. At any rate, I think I gained something by associating with them.

CHAPTER 21

TIME TO SAY GOODBYE

It was the summer of 1978, and I was forty-two years old. My hair was graying rapidly as was the hair on my chest. When Kenji Shibuya and I used to work together in the San Francisco Bay Area, I would put him in a headlock and he would glance up at my chest and comment, "Ah Don, I see snow on the mountain!" Let's face it, I was getting old and probably losing my zest for the business. I had gotten out of coaching after seventeen years which left me teaching English. I wanted to do some counseling and administration to add to my educational resume. In addition, I had an urge to take flight training to earn a private pilot's license.

I was completing a four-week Las Vegas contract which called for Thursday afternoon flights to Vegas with a return that got me back to San Diego at about three thirty a.m. on Friday morning. When I got home, there was a message from the office indicating that I was booked into the Olympic for a big house show Friday night. To be honest, I didn't look forward to working that night but I knew the money would be pretty good. I called the office and confirmed the booking.

I got some much needed sleep that day and left the house at four thirty p.m. for my drive to Los Angeles. On Interstate five, I passed by San Diego's Mission Bay. People were water skiing, barbecuing and, in general, having a great time. What was I doing starting a two and one-half hour drive to work. I think it was then and there I decided to leave the professional wrestling business. I gave my notice that night and two weeks later, I was a retired wrestler.

As I look back, I believe I made the correct decision. The business had been good to me over the years. With some of the money I earned, I entered several financially solid investments and did well. Am I rich? No! Am I wealthy? No! Am I comfortable? Yes! I've seen to it that Dorothy and the kids will receive some financial consideration when I pass on. They won't be rich but they'll know that I was thinking of them.

I was good to the business. In over two thousand bookings, I missed two—one was car trouble; and the other was a miscommunication between the L.A. office and me. I hope I was remembered as a reliable employee.

As I look at the tally sheet, I have to weigh what I gave against what I received in my twenty years of service. I essentially gave some of my body parts—hip, back, shoulder, and elbow. Strangely, I wasn't aware of these problems while I was working. I either overlooked them or "played through" them but now, in my mid-seventies, they haunt me on a daily basis.

On the flip side, what did I gain from the business? I traveled to some super locations, met many outstanding and interesting people, and experienced a multitude of adventures (some good and some not so good) but all contributing to my growth as a person and an entertainer. I think I learned as much about individuals and problems in the wrestling business as I did in my years in education because both fields dealt with attempts to succeed. To me, life is somewhat like flying an airplane—a series of corrections until you reach your destination.

I'm asked occasionally if I would do it again. My answer is yes; I might structure things a bit differently, but I do feel it's been worth it in spite of some of the setbacks. I don't believe there is any such thing as a perfect life, at least to my knowledge. If we do the best we can with the tools we possess, in my opinion, that's living life.

CHAPTER 22

Perspectives

Sometimes when people find out that I was an "old time" professional wrestler, they will ask me my opinion of the current day wrestling business. I have to think about that because we're essentially comparing apples and oranges. Like the rest of the entertainment industry, wrestling has had to keep pace with much of the viewing audience which thrives on action, sex, and violence—not a sparkling endorsement of our society, is it? But, it's true. If we were to give today's wrestling audience one of our hold by hold matches, we would get booed out of the arena with "boring!" These huge kids today have to fly around that ring with high spot after high spot. I marvel at how they can remember all their moves.

The present day wrestling business is fiercely competitive, and if you don't have what it takes to draw and make money for the company, you don't last too long. The work schedule is horrendous. The boys travel to different countries the way we used to travel to different cities. Pro wrestling has become a truly international business.

We told our stories in the ring match by match. Sure, interviews helped to promote big shows but the real content was what we did inside the ropes. I don't watch a lot of wrestling on TV but on occasion I'll tune into a "secret" conversation between personalities who are planning something devious. How can it be a "secret" when a camera man and viewing audience are present—can't figure that one out. Sometimes the expression "soap opera" comes to mind, and the verbal exchanges from the ring to the top of the entrance runway sometimes leave me wondering what they're attempting to accomplish.

Entrance music is nothing new. Gorgeous George, in the 1950's, used to come down the aisle to the strains of "Pomp and Circumstance." It wasn't rock and it wasn't rap, but everyone in the building knew George was on his way to the ring.

Don't get me wrong. I have a tremendous amount of respect for most of the contemporary wrestlers. Many are superior physical specimens and they possess a complete arsenal of match techniques—holds, bumps, the ability to see their opponents' moves, public address skills, and a never ending supply of energy.

Performance enhancement medications: I really don't know a great deal about this activity. The only people I knew who might have been on steroids were some of the serious body builders in the business, and I can't pinpoint that for sure. No one every approached me about drug involvement; it wasn't even talked about in the groups with whom I associated, so, no real comment!

One of my concerns about today's boys in the business is outside the ring bumps. They will be walking the way I do when they get older. The rings they work in are so much better than the old boxing rings we had to deal with. These kids fly off the top rope to the arena floor, and believe me, that floor doesn't give. I don't care how you pad it; it's a virtual slab. Wrestling veteran, John Tolos, once commented to me, "I know I'm taking too many outside bumps when, the next morning, the walk from the bed to the head hurts me." Many times after a fantastic outside bump, the referee will check to see if the boys are okay. Thankfully most of the time they are but after a number of years, they may not be. I wonder if the price is worth it.

The concept of wrestling territories is history. In the "old days" there were several territories spread around the country and the boys, like gypsies, used to move from territory to territory. In most territories, shows were sanctioned by a state athletic commission and we had to pay a licensing fee and undergo medical check-ups according to the rules of a given state's commission. Some states were more stringent than others. California, which was basically my home territory, had a good commission—thorough licensing procedures and they provided a ringside physician at every show.

When a wrestler entered a territory, he knew how long he was going to remain there. However, there was wiggle room for extensions or early departures. Three months was the standard time period for a wrestler's stay in a territory.

There were two major companies in the U.S.: the W.W.A. and the N.W.A., with some small independents (V.W.A.) sprinkled in. The companies weren't really in competition with one another as long as there wasn't territory infringement. The N.W.A. covered the southeastern part of the country and the W.W.A. handled the rest. If a wrestler wanted to move from one company to the other, it wasn't a big deal—give the proper notice and be gone.

It seems that currently Vince McMahon's W.W.E. is pretty much in control of professional wrestling in this country. There are no more territories and I don't know if athletic commissions are involved at all. Years ago, McMahon stated that professional wrestling is now a media event and with so much revenue coming from pay-per-view events, I guess he's right.

For years the wrestling business used to go in popularity cycles—up, then down for a while, and then up again. Vince seems to have kept his version in the spotlight for a number of years. He's smart, organized, and it appears he knows how to run a company.

The small arena shows are essentially a thing of the past along with low admission ticket prices. Now the fans make their signs, pay some good money, and hope to be part of the TV coverage, live or taped.

I hope I haven't been too negative in my comparisons of current professional wrestling and my era of some fifty years ago. I guess almost everything changes over time and the wrestling business is no exception.

CHAPTER 23

Outtakes

In this part of the book, I have related some incidents that kind of stand by themselves. That is, I really didn't know in which chapter to cover them. You be the judge.

Incident: Other than the hard boxing rings, the only other significant threat to my welfare was a few whacko wrestling fans. I was stabbed twice; once in Hampton, Virginia, and once in Los Angeles, California.

The Hampton situation was prefaced by a tag match the week before. The Masked Medic and I (heels) were teamed against Johnny Valentine and Pedro Morales (babyfaces). When I was on the ring apron and Medic was working, some lady would holler obscenities at me and attempt to grab my boots—where's security when you need it. I called her a stupid pig and told her to stay away from me. Next thing I know, this guy about the size of a small building, is standing there asking me if I had called his wife a bitch. I told him no, that I had called her a pig and get her under control. End of incident? No . . .

Evidently, when I left the ring that night, the woman took a swing at me as I turned into the dressing room. She missed and took a bump, skinning her elbows and knees. I wasn't even aware of it because my back was to her. End of incident? No . . .

The following week, Valentine and I returned to Hampton in a single match set up by an angle we shot in the tag event. We had an excellent house and Johnny and I gave them a great show. Following the match, as I was turning into the dressing room, I felt a "thump" on my back. I didn't react because there were a lot of fans leaving the building and I'd been bumped before. Once I was inside the dressing room, some of the boys alerted me about a lot of blood on my back. Someone had put a blade in me creating a puncture wound that missed vital organs but would require medical attention. A man had been detained by security and then released. The whole situation happened so quickly that no one was sure of what had taken place. All I know is that I was on the receiving end of a sharp instrument wielded by an unknown assailant. I wonder who that might have been.

The Los Angeles stabbing occurred at the Olympic Auditorium, and to this day, I can't figure out what actually happened. I was involved in a twenty man battle royal and there were bodies flying everywhere. I had taken a bump through the ropes and was lying face up on the ring apron. I guess my attention was focused on inside the ring action. Then I felt a sharp pain in the front of my left shoulder. Someone had nailed me with a blade. I didn't see it, but I sure did feel it. I could move my left arm so I climbed back into the ring and continued to work until I was eliminated. The wound was superficial and didn't require a lot of attention, just cleaning and bandaging. I must have gotten someone pretty upset to the point of attacking me. Tough business, this professional wrestling!

Incident: I was doing a job for Freddie Blassie at San Diego's Coliseum. Freddie had taken over and was sticking it to me when Jack O'Halloran (Superman I and II) approaches the ring to rescue me. Now Jack is about six feet six inches tall, weighs a good two hundred and forty or fifty pounds, and has had a few drinks. He's bound and determined to enter the ring and come to my aid. At the same time, I have to sell Freddie and counsel Jack out of making a fool of himself, and somehow I managed to do it. Jack retreated and Blassie and I finished our match. After I showered, I ran into Jack at the concession stand and we both joked about the whole situation. Freddie just dismissed it as another night in the ring. It was no big deal.

Incident: I was flying from San Diego to Sacramento to do TV for Roy Shire. In Los Angeles, I changed airplanes but my bag didn't make it from one plane to the other. When I arrived in Sacramento, I searched for my bag with no luck. I was somewhat pressed for time so I journeyed to the TV studio with no wrestling gear. The boys on the card were great. I managed to borrow boots and tights. The tights were too large for me and I didn't have a supporter. I was doing a job for Dutch Savage so I worked as Don Steele. What else could go wrong? When I told Dutch about the loose tights and no supporter, he just roared and said he would "take care" of me. Yeah, sure! On several occasions during our match, I probably should have been arrested for indecent exposure for one reason or another. Even Shire, who never laughed, cracked up.

My bag arrived by cab just as I was leaving the ring so I did have what I needed for my overnight hotel stay. This was a case of better late than never, I guess, and fortunately it was the only time that ever happened to me.

Incident: The Neilson Cure: The Los Angeles territory was dark on New Year's Eve, 1963, but I was scheduled for New Year's day night TV at the Olympic.

Dorothy and I attended a block party on New Year's Eve and I had too many bourbon and sevens—way too many! I went through the whole routine, drunk as a skunk, got sick to my stomach when we got home, was hung over big time on New Year's day to the point I couldn't even get out of bed to watch the Bowl games. My entire body was one big "hurt."

Somehow I managed to get myself together enough for the drive to L.A., but I was still way under the weather when I arrived at the Olympic. I was doing a job for Art Neilson and I told him my plight. Art said he had the perfect hangover cure, and he did. We went about fifteen minutes of non-stop action, up and down, ropes to ropes, bump after bump, working up a real sweat. At the conclusion of the match, I felt one hundred percent better. It's a miracle! I was even hungry on the way back to San Diego and stopped for something to eat. The Art Neilson cure had really worked. Thanks, Art!

CHAPTER 24

Wrap Up

As I look back over my twenty years in the professional wrestling business, I find myself examining the positives and negatives of my experience. Would I want my son or daughter to enter the business—no! Professional wrestling levies harsh demands on one's time, energy, and personal life, depending upon how dedicated an individual is to the business. I took the business seriously and did the best I could to respond to what it was asking of me. In return, the financial reward was fairly good most of the time.

What has to be taken into consideration are the places I traveled, the people I met, and the adventures I experienced because of wrestling—incomparable! I believe most folks in the entertainment industry share that sentiment. Yes, you give a lot, but you can also gain a lot.

ACKNOWLEDGEMENTS

Rick Galyen, who was invaluable with his computer research.

Gina Stevenson, who had to wade through my rough draft to provide a manuscript format.

Rick Galyen and Dale Teschler, who provided critical reads to determine the quality of <u>Carpenter</u>.

Dorothy, my former wife, who put up with me and the wrestling business for thirteen years.

The professional wrestling business, which provided ammunition for much of the book's content.

To our daughter, Karen Cook, whose assistance was vital in publishing CARPENTER.